Senior Seminar on
The Wealth and Well-Being of Nations:

Each year, seniors in the department of economics and management participate in a semester-long course that is built around the ideas and influence of that year's Upton Scholar. By the time the Upton Scholar arrives in October, students will have read several of his or her books and research by other scholars that has been influenced by these writings. This advanced preparation provides students the rare opportunity to engage with a leading intellectual figure on a substantive and scholarly level.

Endowed Student Internship Awards:

A portion of the Miller Upton Memorial Endowments supports exceptional students pursuing high-impact internship experiences. Students are encouraged to pursue internships with for-profit firms and non-profit research organizations dedicated to advancing the wealth and well-being of nations.

Charles G. Koch Student Research Colloquium and Speaker Series:

With generous support from the Charles G. Koch Charitable Foundation, the department has initiated a research colloquium that gives students the opportunity to read and discuss seminal articles aimed at deepening their understanding of the market process. Students also develop original analysis that applies economic ideas to novel contexts. Colloquium participants receive close mentoring as they craft an article with the eventual goal of publication in a newspaper, magazine, or academic journal. The themes of the research colloquium and annual forum are supported with a monthly speaker series featuring the next generation of scholars working on questions central to our understanding of the nature and causes of wealth and well-being.

Annual Proceedings of
The Wealth and Well-Being of Nations:

The keynote address presented by the Upton Scholar is an important contribution to the public discourse on the nature and causes of wealth and well-being. Further, the annual forum includes presentations by noted scholars who expand upon or challenge the work of the Upton Scholar. These presentations are assembled in the *Annual Proceedings of the Wealth and Well-Being of Nations*, which serves as an important intellectual resource for students, alumni, and leaders within higher education.

THE ANNUAL PROCEEDINGS OF THE WEALTH AND WELL-BEING OF NATIONS

2008-2009

VOLUME 1

EMILY CHAMLEE-WRIGHT
EDITOR

JENNIFER KODL
MANAGING EDITOR

CONTENTS

Introduction
    Emily Chamlee-Wright 7

Violence and Social Orders
    Douglass North 19

The Failure to Transplant Democracy, Markets,
    and the Rule of Law into the Developing World
    Barry R. Weingast 29

Institutional Transition and the Problem of Credible Commitment
    Peter Boettke 41

Why Do Elites Permit Reform?
    John V.C. Nye 53

The Importance of Expectations in Economic Development
    Christopher J. Coyne 63

Designing Incentive-Compatible Policies to Promote Human Capital
    Development
    Carolyn J. Heinrich 83

North's Underdeveloped Ideological Entrepreneur
    Virgil Henry Storr 99

Introduction

Emily Chamlee-Wright

As the Elbert Neese Professor of Economics, it is my privilege to introduce the first *Annual Proceedings of the Wealth and Well-Being of Nations*. Under the banner of the Miller Upton Programs, the department of economics and management at Beloit College has launched an ambitious initiative to advance understanding of the ideas and institutions necessary for widespread prosperity and human development. The centerpiece of these programs is the annual Wealth and Well-Being of Nations: a forum in honor of Miller Upton. Every fall, the Upton Forum brings to Beloit College a distinguished, internationally recognized scholar who works within the classical liberal tradition. The Upton Scholar engages with students, faculty, alumni, and civic leaders in an informed dialogue around the nature and causes of wealth and well-being. In 2008, we were honored to feature Douglass North, Spencer T. Olin Professor in Arts and Sciences at Washington University in St. Louis and co-recipient of the 1993 Nobel Memorial Prize in Economic Sciences as the inaugural Upton Scholar.

During the week of the Upton Forum, we assembled leading scholars who have advanced Professor North's intellectual project by extending his ideas into new territory—territory that even Professor North may not have originally considered. We assembled this cadre of scholars to demonstrate that, despite the momentous advances made by our Upton Scholar, the intellectual enterprise of understanding the nature and causes of wealth and well-being is an ongoing project. The essays collected in this volume capture in written form many of the ideas exchanged, challenges posed, and questions considered over the course of the Upton Forum.

Before introducing Professor North and the substance of the contributions made within this volume, let me say a few words about the man for whom the forum is named. R. Miller Upton was the sixth president of Beloit College and served from 1954 to 1975. A nationally recognized leader in higher education, President Upton was known to harbor two intellectual passions. The first was a steadfast commitment to the liberal arts. He believed that the small residential liberal arts college was the ideal place to engage the "great questions," as it is here that students are expected to acquire the intellectual habits necessary for critical thinking and open civil discourse. His second passion was for the ideals of the liberal society: political freedom, the rule of law, and the promotion of peace and prosperity through the voluntary exchange of goods, services, and ideas. He understood that transforming the ideals of liberal democracy into real institutions was at the heart of increasing the wealth and well-being of nations and peoples. We believe that the Upton Forum represents a confluence where these enduring passions meet.

A Life of Intellectual Discovery

Let me turn now to formally introducing our inaugural Upton Scholar, Douglass North. As I have already mentioned, Professor North is the co-recipient of the 1993 Nobel Prize in Economics. I would like to offer a brief sketch as to why this scholar's work has been worthy of such an honor and how it has changed the nature of the economics discipline.

The best place to begin is with the phrase "social institutions." It is, after all, his research on the evolution of social institutions and the impact social institutions have had on economic performance over time for which Professor North received the Nobel Prize. And the best way to explain the relevance of social institutions is to draw upon a familiar metaphor.

Think of society as a game. There are many versions of the social game. There is the market game, the game we call "family," and the game we call "politics," just to name a few. Like any game of sport, these games are played according to a specific set of rules. Some of these rules are formal and can be written down. Others rules (or what we might call "social norms") are less formal but are every bit as real as their more formal counterparts. And for the rules to work, there has to be some kind of enforcement, which again, might be formal in nature, like a referee, or informal, as in the social sanctions imposed by your teammates for poor sportsmanship. In any game of sport, formal rules, informal norms, and enforcement mechanisms govern individual behavior and provide a structure within which individuals interact with one another.

Similarly, social institutions are the rules, norms, and enforcement mechanisms that govern individual behavior and structure social interactions within the market, within families, within politics, and so on.

In the early part of his career, Professor North focused on eighteenth- and nineteenth-century American economic growth and the use of quantitative economic analysis in interpreting historical change (North 1966). But as he sought to address the deeper root causes of economic performance and change in the United States and Europe, such as the monumental social and economic changes that occurred as Europe transitioned from medieval to modern times, he began to realize that the standard tools of economics were not up to the task of explaining these fundamental changes (North 1971; North and Thomas 1973). Anyone who has taken even an introductory course in economics knows something about these standard tools of what we call neoclassical economic theory. These tools can be marvelously clarifying if you are trying to understand how, for example, prices coordinate the actions of producers and consumers. But notice that such explanations assume the rules of the game—such as private property, money, and rules of exchange—are already in place.

Further, because standard economic analysis assumes that engaging in market exchange is costless—that there are no costs associated with measuring quality, monitoring performance, holding people to the bargains they strike—most standard models did not have to consider the role of social institutions. But in the world in which we *live*, it is often very costly to monitor the performance of employees, we are often quite uncertain about the quality of goods and services we purchase, and we worry considerably about whether promises others make to us will be honored. In the real world, we have employee bonus incentives, we have laws against consumer fraud, and we have contracts that bind parties to agreements and courts that will uphold those contracts. These are among the rules of the game—the social institutions—that make the market work. Professor North recognized that if we wanted to understand *how* social institutions work and how they evolve and change, we would need new tools.

In the course of his investigations of American and European economic history, Professor North improved upon neoclassical theory by adding in tools of new institutional analysis that would allow us to understand social change. But questions remained, or as Professor North describes them, there were still "loose ends that did not make sense."[1] If some institutional arrangements are clearly better than others at expanding wealth, he wondered, why do inefficient institutional arrangements often hang on for long periods of time? Soviet-style socialism, for example, was surely inefficient, but it hung on for more than seventy years. Why didn't Soviet citizens and leaders abandon such arrangements as we would expect a factory owner to abandon an inefficient production process? Neoclassical economics could help us understand the perverse incentives of political actors, but another factor still seemed to be in play: the role played by ideology or shared belief systems and how politics, ideology, and institutional arrangements each influenced the other (North 1981).

Ideology can act like a kind of glue that gives institutions sticking power. This institutional stickiness can be a very good thing when it reinforces rules such as the private property rights that are so important to economic progress. Think about the many ways we promote ideological support for property. It is woven through our moral and legal code, our religious doctrine, our educational system, and our habits of parenting. The effect of all this ideological investment is to lower the costs of enforcing private property rights, thereby fostering productivity, efficiency, and civility.

But ideological stick can work the other way as well. Sometimes societies get tracked into ideological commitments that make society less productive, less efficient, and less civil. Why? According to the rationality postulate economists assert, this shouldn't be so, and yet it often is. Perhaps, Professor North considered, rationality is far less important in explaining the choices people make (particularly under conditions of uncertainty and when informational feedback is weak) than we thought (North 1990). Perhaps it is what people *believe* to be true, how they learn and update what they know based on that initial set of beliefs, rather than what from a rationalist's perspective *is* true that directs the evolutionary course of social change over long periods of time. If that is the case, Professor North concluded, economists will have to retool again, this time by diving deeply into the tools of cognitive science to understand the ways in which the human mind learns (or fails to learn), how we succeed in correcting (or fail to correct) our course toward belief systems that foster greater efficiency and

---

[1] See Professor North's autobiographical statement on the Nobel Prize website http://nobelprize. org/nobel_prizes/economics/laureates/1993/north-autobio.html

civility, or in other words, toward belief systems that foster wealth and well-being (North 2005).

Most recently, Professor North has turned his attention to understanding the evolutionary process by which the liberal democratic order is obtained. Political philosophers, social scientists, and development policy consultants have long assumed, and understandably so, that reforms aimed at introducing market competition and eliminating public corruption would be necessary if societies were to enjoy the fruits of the liberal democratic order. But the sometimes disappointing record of post-Soviet reforms and the many decades of failed attempts to introduce liberal reforms in much of the developing world suggest that a successful transition is anything but certain. And the fact that only a handful of societies can claim to have made this transition successfully suggests an intriguing question of *how* this success is won.

In his latest book, *Violence and Social Orders: A Conceptual Framework for Interpreting Recorded Human History*, published in 2009, Professor North and his co-authors Barry Weingast and John Wallis take on this question, first by considering the systematic qualities of the pre-modern state—what they call the "natural state." Most civilizations throughout human history (including most contemporary societies) are best described as natural states, in which rulers create social order by restricting access to political and economic markets to a privileged elite. While this form of social order has the evolutionary benefit of limiting violence, it also limits the potential for economic prosperity. Liberal democratic, or "open access," societies, on the other hand, create order by fostering market and political competition. Professor North and his co-authors argue that by understanding the inherent logic of the limited access order, we are in a far better position to understand the evolutionary process that is required for societies to make a successful transition to an open access society. It is this line of research that Professor North considers in his keynote address, with particular emphasis on the implications this interpretive framework has for understanding our contemporary political and economic circumstances.

In this brief introduction there is no way that I can do justice to the nuance and particular care with which Professor North presents these ideas, but what I hope I *have* done is to give the reader some sense of the intellectual character of this scholar. He pays careful attention to the tools of economic theory that had been passed down to see what puzzles they can solve. When he comes upon the limits of these tools, he doesn't throw up his hands and say, "If our tools can't handle the question, it must not be worth asking." Instead he doggedly pursues the question by fashioning new tools. The good questions he has asked have led to even better (and more difficult) questions that have required interdisciplinary inquiry. Such inquiry was not an abandonment of economics: it was an enrichment of economics. This exemplifies the intellectual character we promote here at Beloit; one that balances disciplinary grounding with interdisciplinary discovery; one that fosters open discourse with equal measures of intellectual passion and civility. It is therefore fitting that a scholar who exemplifies so well these qualities should be our inaugural Upton Scholar.

Discovery in Conversation

If discovery is the principal goal of scholarship, then the conversations it creates are its principal side benefit. Sometimes our partners in these conversations are friends, sometimes foes, but either way, the best conversations are those that make us think hard and discover more. Like President Upton, we believe that the liberal arts college is the perfect venue to model discovery through engaged civil discourse and to advance its principles by readying our students for a life of the mind; a life that is firmly planted in the world, but one that is unapologetically intellectual. With this purpose in mind, we were honored to feature some of the key scholars who have participated in the conversations that Professor North had a hand in creating.

Barry R. Weingast is the Ward C. Krebs Family Professor of Political Science at Stanford University and senior fellow at the Hoover Institution. Professor Weingast's research focuses on the political determinants of public policymaking and the political foundations of markets and democracy. During the course of their careers, Professors North and Weingast have had many opportunities to collaborate with one another, including co-authorship of what is now considered a seminal article on the relationship between constitutional constraints and economic growth (North and Weingast 1989). In his keynote address, Professor North was able to describe their most recent collaborative effort and its implications for contemporary political and economic life. In his contribution, Professor Weingast focuses on the transition from "personalistic" and impermanent political rules to impersonal and perpetual rules that do not depend upon the particular personalities who hold power. Professor Weingast argues that prevailing economic wisdom has failed to generate effective reforms because economists and reformers have failed to understand the connection between political privilege and social order within natural states.

Peter Boettke is BB&T Professor for the Study of Capitalism, at the Mercatus Center at George Mason University and a University Professor at George Mason University. Professor Boettke is the author of several books on the history, collapse, and transition from socialism in the former Soviet Union (Boettke 1990, 1993, 2001). As a leading contributor to our understanding of why Soviet-type systems fail to generate widespread economic well-being, Professor Boettke is perfectly positioned to shed light on what has gone right and what has gone wrong in the process of post-Soviet reform. In the contribution he offers here, Professor Boettke examines the lessons learned in this (still continuing) process. In particular, he emphasizes the importance of establishing binding and credible commitments to liberal limits on state action if societies are to avoid suffering the disastrous consequences of illiberal democracy and severely distorted and hampered market economies.

John Nye holds the Frederic Bastiat Chair in Political Economy at the Mercatus Center and is a professor of economics at George Mason University. Before accepting his position at George Mason, Professor Nye had been a long-time colleague of Professor North at Washington University. He is a specialist in British and French economic history and in new institutional economics. His recent book, *War, Wine, and Taxes: the Political Economy of Anglo-French Trade 1689–1900* (2007), challenges the conventional wisdom that nineteenth-century Britain was an icon of free trade. In the essay Professor Nye offers here, he examines the question of why elites within pre-modern or natural states, who earn economic rents[2] and other forms of political privilege from the status quo, ever consent to reform.

Christopher Coyne is assistant professor of economics at West Virginia University. In his book *After War: The Political Economy of Exporting Democracy*

---

[2] The phrase "economic rent" refers to a return captured by someone who possesses an exclusive and valuable position within society. Economic rent can come from possessing a valuable and difficult to emulate talent (such as the clear tones of an operatic virtuoso), or it can come from possessing some exclusive political advantage (such as the exclusive or protected right to operate within a particular industry). It is this latter source of economic rent that fascinates and troubles economists, as rents and the seeking of politically created rents tend to foster behaviors that stifle economic and human progress. For a full discussion, see Gordon Tullock's *The Rent Seeking Society* (2005).

(2007), Professor Coyne deploys the economic way of thinking to shed light on why the West has had such a poor record of success in its attempts at "nation building" around the world. Insights drawn from Professor North's work are critical in this assessment. In the essay he contributes here, Professor Coyne examines the implications Professor North's latest work has for international development assistance programs. He argues that specialists working within development agencies tend to hold and perpetuate naively optimistic expectations regarding the effectiveness of their programs because they fail to consider the inherent constraints of operating within the context of a limited access society. Professor Coyne argues further that such expectations can lead to perverse economic outcomes and the failure of development efforts.

Among those invited to present their work at the Upton Forum are distinguished alumni scholars. And given our department's focus on the social institutions necessary for widespread wealth and well-being and entrepreneurship as the driving force behind human progress, it is not surprising that we have alumni scholars doing work within the intellectual tradition of our Upton Scholar.

Carolyn Heinrich ('89) is director of the La Follette School of Public Affairs and professor of public affairs at the University of Wisconsin–Madison. She is co-author of several books on the empirical study of governance and public management, including *Improving Governance: A New Logic for Empirical Research* (2002) and *Governance and Performance: New Perspectives* (2000). Professor Heinrich works directly with both state and national governments assessing programs aimed at human capital development, such as conditional cash transfer programs designed to increase school attendance in the developing world and the provision of supplemental education services in the United States. Based on the insights drawn from the new institutionalist school of economics, such programs are generally seen as possessing tremendous potential as they aim to align incentives between the intended outcomes and program participants. In the essay she contributes to this volume, Professor Heinrich considers both this potential and also the difficulties involved in keeping incentives aligned once the program is implemented on the ground.

Virgil Storr ('96) is a senior research fellow and the director of graduate student programs at the Mercatus Center and the Don C. Lavoie Research Fellow in the Program in Philosophy, Politics, and Economics in the department of economics at George Mason University. Dr. Storr's research emphasizes the connections between culture, political-economy, and entrepreneurship. He is the author of *Enterprising Slaves & Master Pirates* (2004), in which he examines the intersection of cultural and economic life in the Bahamas. I have had the great privilege of serving as co-investigator with Dr. Storr on the Mercatus Center's project on Gulf Coast recovery following Hurricane Katrina. In this research, we examine the role socially and culturally embedded resources play as residents, business owners, and social entrepreneurs attempt to facilitate community rebound (Chamlee-Wright and Storr 2009a; 2009b; 2009c). In the essay Dr. Storr contributes here, he examines what he identifies as an underdeveloped concept within Professor North's work; that of the "ideological entrepreneur." Ideological entrepreneurs are those who change institutional structure by cultivating a shift in shared ideology. Dr. Storr argues that as a driving force behind social change, the figure of the ideological entrepreneur requires further development, which he offers by bridging North's concept to the theories of entrepreneurship advanced by Israel Kirzner and Joseph Schumpeter.

The essays contained within this volume serve as a pointed reminder of the power of ideas in shaping the world. At least from the perspective of this political-economist, it was ideas that shaped the course of human history in the twentieth century, and I expect that this will be no less true in the century we are living in now. Thus, the content of those ideas matters a great deal if we are to understand where we have been and where we are headed. Further, this collection represents a modest but still profound statement of how ideas are advanced—through considered, engaged, and passionate discourse. Preparing students for a life of the mind in which this is regular practice is the enduring and distinctive promise of a liberal education.

With Many Thanks

On behalf of Jeff Adams, the Allen-Bradley Professor of Economics, and the other members of the department of economics and management, I want to extend our thanks to everyone who has played a part in making the Upton Forum and associated programs a reality. Through their financial support, exceptionally good counsel, and willingness to serve as campaign chairs for the Miller Upton Memorial Endowments, Bill Fitzgerald ('86) and Bob Virgil ('56) laid the foundation for this initiative, ensuring that it would serve as a fitting memorial to Miller and provide a signature experience for Beloit College students for many years to come. As the former dean of the business school at Washington

University and longtime friend to Douglass North, Bob Virgil was also instrumental in securing the participation of Professor North as our inaugural Upton Scholar.

I would also like to thank the many scholars and alumni professionals who presented at the 2008 forum. In addition to the contributors to this volume, I would like to thank, James Herbison ('96), Daniel Hewitt ('78), Jeffrey Kuster ('88), and Wendy Olsen ('82)[3] for participating in the forum events. Thanks also go to the students who worked extremely hard to prepare themselves for the discussions in which they participated. In particular, the members of the 2008 Senior Seminar in Economics are to be commended for their enthusiasm in reading and discussing many books and academic articles by Professor North and our other visiting scholars prior to the forum. Special thanks also go to Jennifer Kodl, managing editor of the *Annual Proceedings* and conference coordinator for the Upton Forum, whose dedication to gracious excellence stands as a model for us all (faculty and student alike) to emulate.

Finally, we would like to thank the Lynde and Harry Bradley Foundation, the Neese Family Foundation, Inc., and the Charles G. Koch Charitable Foundation. Not only have these organizations provided generous financial support to this effort, the people who make these organizations run have also provided inspiration and valuable guidance. Special thanks go to Janet Riordan, Gary Grabowski, Ryan Stowers, and Jayme Lemke.

References

Boettke, Peter. 1990. *The Political Economy of Soviet Socialism: The Formative Years, 1918–1928*. New York: Springer.

_____. 1993. *Why Perestroika Failed: The Economics and Politics of Socialism Transformation*. London: Routledge.

_____. 2001. *Calculation and Coordination: Essays on Socialism and Transitional Political Economy*. London: Routledge.

Chamlee-Wright, Emily and Virgil Henry Storr. 2009a. Club Goods and Post-disaster Community Return. *Rationality & Society* 21(4): 1–30.

---

[3] During the alumni panels, Dr. Olsen presented her paper "Moral Political Economy and Moral Reasoning about Rural India," to appear in a forthcoming edition of the *Cambridge Journal of Economics*.

_____. 2009b. The Role of Social Entrepreneurship in Community Recovery. *International Journal of Innovation and Regional Development*. (Forthcoming).

_____. 2009c. "There's No Place Like New Orleans": Sense of Place and Community Recovery in the Ninth Ward After Hurricane Katrina. *Journal of Urban Affairs*. (Forthcoming).

Coyne, Christopher. 2007. *After War: The Political Economy of Exporting Democracy*. Stanford: Stanford University Press.

Heinrich, Carolyn and Laurence Lynn. 2000. *Governance and Performance: New Perspectives*. Washington D.C.: Georgetown University Press.

Lynn, Laurence, Carolyn Heinrich, and Carolyn Hill. 2002. *Improving Governance: A New Logic for Empirical Research*. Washington D.C.: Georgetown University Press.

North, Douglass C. 1966. *The Economic Growth of the United States: 1790–1860*. New York: W.W. Norton.

_____ 1971. *Institutional Change and American Economic Growth*. Cambridge: Cambridge University Press.

_____ 1981. *Structure and Change in Economic History*. New York: W.W. Norton.

_____ 1990. *Institutions, Institutional Change, and Economic Performance*. Cambridge: Cambridge University Press.

_____ 2005. *Understanding the Process of Economic Change*. Princeton: Princeton University Press.

North, Douglass C. and Robert Thomas. 1973. *The Rise of the Western World: A New Economic History*. Cambridge: Cambridge University Press.

North, Douglass C., John Wallis, and Barry Weingast. 2009. *Violence and Social Orders: A Conceptual Framework for Interpreting Recorded Human History*. Cambridge: Cambridge University Press.

North, Douglass C. and Barry Weingast. 1989. Constitutions and Commitment: The Evolution of Institutions Governing Public Choice in 17th Century England. *Journal of Economic History* 49(4): 803–832.

Nye, John. 2007. *War, Wine, and Taxes: the Political Economy of Anglo-French Trade 1689–1900*. Princeton: Princeton University Press.

Storr, Virgil H. 2004. *Enterprising Slaves & Master Pirates*. New York: Peter Lang.

Tullock, Gordon. 2005. *The Rent Seeking Society*. Ed. Charles K. Rowley. Indianapolis: Liberty Fund.

Violence and Social Orders

Douglass North[*][1]

It is a great honor and a pleasure to be the inaugural Upton Scholar. During my residency, I have come to appreciate not only Miller Upton but Beloit College, and I am delighted to be here.

I am going to present here a very brief summary of a new book I and two co–authors, Barry Weingast, professor of political science at Stanford University, and John Wallis, professor of economics at the University of Maryland, have just finished. We have attempted to develop an entirely new approach to understanding how a society evolves through time.

After the summary, which I will attempt to make precise, I want to consider some of the implications of the book not only for rethinking the past, which a lot of this book is concerned with, but also for thinking about the present and the future and what we ought to be doing in the social sciences.

The title of our book is *Violence and Social Orders: a Conceptual Framework for Interpreting Recorded Human History*. That is a really modest title—designed to disarm. It was chosen deliberately because we wanted to rethink the fundamentals of how society has evolved through time.

The human world has undergone two dramatic social revolutions, both producing fundamental changes in the stock of knowledge. The first began ten

[*] Douglass North is Spencer T. Olin Professor in Arts and Sciences at Washington University in St. Louis and the co-recipient of the 1993 Nobel Memorial Prize in Economic Sciences. Professor North served as the 2008 Upton Scholar during the Wealth and Well-Being of Nations annual forum at Beloit College.

[1] I would like to thank Emily Chamlee-Wright for her kind introduction and the many people responsible for launching the Miller Upton Forum. In particular, I would like to thank my long-time friend Bob Virgil for playing a central role in establishing this wonderful program.

thousand years ago with the discovery of agriculture and the growth of larger societies, the first cities, and the emergence of hierarchical social organization. The second began about 250 years ago with the development of new industrial technologies, the rise of nation states and the emergence of new and sophisticated political and economic organizations.

The two revolutions each led to new ways of organizing human interaction and ordering society. Our conceptual framework lays out the logic underlying the two new social orders and the process by which societies made the transition from one to the other. After laying out the conceptual framework, we consider the logic of the social order that appeared ten millennia ago—what we call the limited access society or the natural state. Natural states used the political system to regulate economic competition and create economic rents. It then used these rents to order social relationships, control violence, and establish social cooperation.

The natural state transformed human history. Indeed, the first natural states developed the techniques of building and recording that resulted in the beginning of recorded human history. Most of the world today still lives in natural states.

Next, we consider the logic of the social order that emerged in a few societies at the end of the eighteenth and beginning of the nineteenth centuries, what we call open access societies. As with the appearance of natural states, open access societies transformed human history in a fundamental way. Perhaps twenty-five countries and maybe fifteen percent of the world's population live in open access societies, and the rest, about eighty-five percent of the world, live in natural states still. Open access societies regulate economic competition in a way that dissipates rents and uses competition to order social relationships. The third task of the book is to explain how societies make the transition from one to the other.

I want to elaborate on the conceptual framework. In the primitive social order that preceded the natural state, human interaction occurs mainly through repeated face-to-face interaction, and all relationships are personal. The typical size unit of human interaction is the band of about twenty-five people. The level of violence within and between groups is very high.

The natural state provided a solution to violence by embedding powerful members of society in a coalition of military, political, religious, and economic elites. Elites all possessed special privileges, access to valuable resources or valuable activities and the ability to form organizations. Limited access to activities, organizations, and privileges produce rents for the elites. Because these rents are reduced if violence breaks out, rent creation enabled elites to credibly commit to each other to limit violence. Violence plays a role all through our discussion: we think that the threat of violence all through history has dominated the way in which societies have tried to deal with organization and cooperation.

Natural states are stable but not static. In comparison with primitive order, limited access orders—natural states—significantly expanded the size of societies. Hierarchies of elites built personal relationships that extended the control of the dominant coalition. Personal relationships in natural states resulted from tradi-tional face-to-face interaction. In well-developed natural states, elite privileges included control over powerful social organizations such as a church, govern-ment, courts, and military units.

Open access orders, built on the organizational achievements of the natural state, extend citizenship to an ever-growing proportion of the population. All citizens are able to form economic, political, religious, or social organizations to produce any number of functions. The only proscribed function is the use of violence. Unlike the natural state, which actively manipulates the interests of elites and non-elites to ensure social order, the open access society allows indi-viduals to pursue their own interests through active competition. Individuals continue to be motivated by economic rents in both political and economic markets.

In an open access society, social order is maintained through the interaction of competition, institutions, and beliefs. Control of the military is concentrated in government, and control over the government is subject both to political competition and institutional constraints. Attempts to use government to coerce citizens, either directly through the use of military force or indirectly through manipulation of economic interests, result in the activation of existing orga-nizations or creation of new organizations that mobilize economic and social resources to establish control over the political system.

I want to review the above in noneconomic terms. We think there are two fundamental ways that human beings in the last ten thousand years have orga-nized society. In one, a small percentage of the population are elites. They control a system, whether in political, religious, or economic organizations. They capture most of the gains of the society and so the rest of the society are generally second-class citizens—slaves, serfs, or just persons with no particular property rights. This way of organization has dominated and still dominates the world. More than eighty percent of the world's population still lives in such societies. Open access is a new development. It rests upon competition in political and economic markets, and it particularly rests on bringing greater and greater proportions of the population to becoming participating citizens with equal rights. The fundamental difference, of course, is that in the limited access society—the natural state—personal relationships and who you are and whom you know count.

In open access society there are property rights and impersonal exchange; who you are is less important than what you do and what you can do. This impersonal exchange has opened up by competition driving forces that have encouraged enormous expansions in economic growth and prosperity in the modern world. A rich society is a result of an open access society.

The question arises, how does a transition occur? The transition is a problem because limited access societies are societies in which elites run the systems. They are a small proportion of the population—ten, fifteen, twenty percent at the most—but they are getting all the benefits and, obviously, anything that changes or undermines them is something they would not welcome. Open access societies are just the reverse. They are competitive. Competition dominates the way in which both political and economic markets work. The economy works by innovative creation; there is competition in markets, and those players who create more efficient, productive methods stand to gain and replace those who are less efficient. Innovation and creativity are the heart of what makes markets work and what has made the modern world so dynamic and such an extraordinary place.

How do you get from the limited to open access? It is not easy. Most of the world is still a natural state and still lives with very incomplete and imperfect forms of economic, political, and social organizations; the great percentage of the population play no part in the way in which their societies are run. What would ever move a society from one to the other? We argue in our book that there gradually emerged conditions that made it in the self-interest of the elites to move toward open access. We call these doorstep conditions and contend that there are three of them.

The first doorstep condition is that elites extended property rights beyond themselves to a broader group of the population. Why would they do that? They do that if markets are expanding and if they can gain by extending privileges further and further. Let me illustrate by way of an historical example. In the fifteenth to sixteenth century, England began developing overseas with organizations such as the East India Company. The elites found that if they extended the markets so that they allowed other people beyond the elites to buy shares in the stock, they could enormously increase the output and increase the income they could derive and the capital they could use to expand what they were doing.

The second doorstep condition was the allowing of a growth of a broader array of organizations and institutions that could take advantage of the new opportunities that arose as a result of the first condition. The organizations had to have some degree of independence and, in particular, they had to have perpetual life. Perpetual life in a world where you had only personal exchange is obviously a contradiction in terms. In personal exchange, when the person who runs the organization dies the organization also dies. Necessary, therefore, was the evolution of institutional arrangements in organizations that would make possible the creation of a broader set of opportunities and therefore broader participation. Organizations took on a life of their own and began to build policies and activities outside the narrow confines of the elites themselves.

The third condition was that the military gradually broke out from being under control of the elites and came under independent control so that it would not be a tool for the elites to use in retaining power. I know from personal experience how common the use of this tool is. As an advisor to Latin American countries I have seen that every time a ruling elite got into trouble, they would call in the military, create a dictatorship, and recreate the old system of political and economic rents. Wresting control of the military from the grip of the elites is a particularly difficult but essential doorstep condition to achieve.

All three of those conditions have to be occurring if a society is to move beyond the natural state. This confluence does not occur very often. When it does occur, the result is the gradual creation of a whole new world—the world of open access. The dominant feature of open access is that "who you are" becomes less important. Much more important are the rules of the game, well-defined property rights, and the judicial systems at work. Their creation is a long and difficult process.

I also know this from personal experience. I am an advisor to half a dozen countries around the world. All of them are limited access societies or natural states. As an advisor also to the World Bank, I have watched the Bank attempting to change these societies into open access ones. The attempts fail; the Bank has spent about $125 billion failing. The reason is very straightforward. The policies the Bank encourages are policies that work in open access societies: competition, free markets, property rights that are secure. In a limited access society, in which the doorstep conditions are not fulfilled, policies that work in open access societies undermine the very security of the elites. Violence becomes the order of the day. The problem is evident in Iraq today. Iraq is a classic case of having broken down a limited access society and not having replaced it with anything, and we are in the midst of trying to figure out how to deal with such a situation—not very effectively, I might add.

Now, what all this has to say is that the whole way we have thought about economic activity and economic organization has been wrong. It has been wrong because it does not encourage growth. For example, if you want to improve the prospects of poor countries in the world, you do not want to use the tools of an open access society, such as secure property rights, which you cannot put into place overnight. What you want to do is move limited access societies to become more and more secure and move them up to fulfill doorstep conditions. That is a long road. Trying to create democracy in Iraq—a society that is nowhere near being ready for such activities—has been a disaster.

Aid policies have made a mistake in what we have been trying to do because we have misunderstood the very nature of what makes for social order in limited access societies. In such societies, order is maintained by the elites interacting with each other and not getting into conflict, and that requires cooperation. Once you break down the structure without replacing it or without creating the conditions that would move you into a more advanced kind of competitive society, you get violence and disorder.

How do we produce results that will create development in limited access societies that moves them from being fragile to stable natural states? A fragile natural state is one that has just emerged from having violence be dominant and has replaced it with a set of institutions that allow it very gradually to maintain order. A more stable natural state is one in which institutions gradually develop that widen the horizons of the players to include ways of having specialization and division of labor and gradually build up a more complex structure.

A mature natural state is one like Mexico, which has developed quite complex structures, including a number of organizations that are independent of government control and personal exchange, but in which the dominant structure is still personal interaction of the elites.

We have tried to persuade the World Bank, I think successfully in the last few years, that it must rethink how to improve society's development, rethink the characteristics of an open access society versus a natural state or limited access society and how they work. And once you have understood the institutional and organizational structure of the societies, then ask yourself how incrementally you can make them work better. That is what we are trying to do.

Now, that is a very brief summary. What are the implications? The place to begin is to recognize that we live in a dynamic world. One of the real limitations of economics is that it has an enormously powerful set of tools to look at how a market or economy works at a moment in time but not over time.

Our interest is in a dynamic world, a world that is continually changing. The movement within the natural state (from fragile to stable to mature) and then of the doorstep conditions to the modern, open access society means a continual evolution. But it is more complicated than that, which is the reason we get into so much trouble as economists when we give advice. Every society is different. Every society evolves its own culture. It has its own beliefs, its own experiences, its own institutions, and as they have evolved, therefore, they are unique. If you try to uniformly apply what worked in country A to country B, you are going to get in trouble. It is not going to work the same way because beliefs and institutions are going to be different in each society. Indeed, I have a general rule: before I go to advise a country, I spend six months reading about its culture, history, and beliefs so that I can understand what makes it tick. I do not give advice to any country until I have done that.

That is a very expensive and time-consuming effort and it keeps me into mischief trying to keep up with all of it; but nevertheless it is a way to think intelligently about the process of change. Economic advice so often is wrong because it says generalizations can be applied anywhere and they work. That is just simply not true.

My last point here is that it is a non-ergotic world. An ergotic world would be one in which the fundamental underlying structure is uniform and exists everywhere. In such a world, if you understand that fundamental underlying structure and you want to solve a new problem, you go back to fundamentals and then build your theory based on the structure. Now that is what is done in the physical sciences and the natural sciences. The social sciences, however, have no such tools; and, what is much more difficult—the world just keeps changing. The fundamentals that made the United States the country that it is today are fine today, but they are not going to work tomorrow. Now, this should not surprise you because if you look at your own life and the changes that have occurred in your own history, you realize the economy and social order of twenty or thirty years ago are not what they are today.

To take one simple illustration: information costs have been revolutionized in the world. So revolutionized that everything we do is transformed with respect to the speed and the form of communication. The result is a completely new world. Now, this poses a real dilemma for us because the theory we have to deal with our economy today is a theory that was predicated on what worked. In fact, economists have created elaborate models of how the economy worked. To the degree the economy stays the same, the models may work very well. But how long are they going to stay working that way? A few general points underlie what I am asserting. The way in which we understand the world is subjective. We get impulses through our eyes, ears, nose and feelings, and these go into the brain, and there, the brain has to make sense out of them. Cognitive science, which is the place we should begin all intelligent and interesting structure in the social sciences, attempts to understand how the brain takes and organizes impulses so we can translate them into making sense of the world we live in.

Note the implications of what I am saying. It means that the way I understand the world is not only going to be different from the way you understand the world, but it is going to be very different from the way in which a Papuan in New Guinea understands the world. Why? Because the different experiences we all have had are going to be so different that they have built up a whole new understanding of the world around us that will be absolutely different in New Guinea than it is in the United States.

Now, before you despair with that, note that culture here plays a crucial role. Culture connects the past with the present. Much of our belief system, therefore, has evolved, and so we can have a culture that has some degree of coherence to it.

That is fine, but do not forget that as we keep changing, the culture keeps changing; the belief systems underlying it are changing because we are getting new experiences. The first order of business we have is to understand the whole way by which human beings understand and build a set of relationships—the way in which their experiences get translated into a belief system which in turn then translates into a set of institutions.

We then try to order them in such a way that we can make sense out of the world and have it run the way we want it to with the ever-present possibility of disorder and violence being a crucial dilemma. What we have first is belief systems, which then translate into creating institutions, but even that is complicated because institutions are rules, norms, social order, and enforcement characteristics.

Economic institutions—property rights and other social rules that we talk about in economics—are derivative of political institutions. The political system defines the kind of economic rules of the game and the judicial system you have. All that makes for a very complicated story. All of that will be understood very imperfectly, and even if we do understand it today, it will change tomorrow.

The process of surviving in the world we live in not only means that we must understand the world, but as it keeps evolving, we must keep on changing our understanding and adjusting so that we can keep up with it—a very complex process, always imperfectly done. With different experiences in the Islamic society, to take the classic modern illustration, from Western society, we produce differences of views, conflict, disorder, and warfare. We have not solved any of those problems. We have a dynamic system that is evolving. It is evolving very imperfectly. And to the degree that we understand it at all, we understand it very imperfectly.

We have done well enough in the last two hundred years to create societies, like the United States, with a degree of order and structure to produce levels of well-being that were unimaginable in the past. We have done very well in a small part of the world, in open access societies that are maybe fifteen to twenty percent of the world's population. However, the rest of the world is still left behind and is finding it very difficult to move into an open access society.

Moreover, we are continually faced by the fact that our world is changing so rapidly that we have to employ adaptive efficiency to keep up with it. What we mean by adaptive efficiency is that we create an institutional framework that encourages experimentation when we run into new problems, such as the financial crisis we face today. Since the problems are new and novel, we do not have a theory to explain them, so we experiment with new ideas, new policy measures, and new intuitional arrangements.

You want to have institutions that encourage experimentation. You also want to have a structure that eliminates failures. Bankruptcy laws are a good example of a structure that helps markets weed out commercial failures. Similarly, in order to function properly, a society must have a way to eliminate failed political experiments. But when we create policies, organizations, and institutions to address new problems, we also create vested interests, and there will be attempts to perpetuate them even if the new structure does not work well. I am painting for you a complex story. It is an ongoing dilemma of how you deal with a world that continually evolves like this.

What are some of the implications of this story for the world we live in today? The most obvious one is that we live in an open access society. Is it going to continue to be open access? Does it threaten to fall back into being a limited access society? That is an ever-present threat. How stable is the system that we have? How likely is it to persist? What kinds of rules can we make and what kinds of policies can we pursue that will encourage its persistence?

My story can be related to the present world. We are facing a fundamental financial crisis. It is a financial crisis that our economists like to say looks like the 1930s or maybe 1990. It has some similarities, but the beginning of wisdom is to recognize that in the 1930s, the world was a very simple world. The institutions and organizations it had—how they worked, how they operated, what made them work—were completely different from those in the world in which we live. It did not have derivatives. It did not have the institutional arrangements that have fostered both the complexity and instability we are experiencing presently. Today we grope to make sense out of this world so that we can deal with it. We are still engaging in adaptive efficiency.

We are going to try a lot of things. Most of the things we have done so far, I might add, are not going to work very well. We will try things, and eventually, something will work better and we will get somewhere. It is an ongoing process. It requires that we maintain adaptive efficiency, that we do not cut off alternatives that are promising; all of that is making for a world that is very complex.

It is a very exciting world.

The Failure to Transplant Democracy, Markets, and the Rule of Law into the Developing World

Barry R. Weingast[*]

1. Introduction

Why has it proven so difficult to promote democracy, markets, and the rule of law in developing countries? Reformers of all stripes have proposed plans to promote these elements around the world, across different continents and cultures; and each year development agencies promote plans for a wide range of countries.

To address this question, I draw on my recent work with Professors Douglass North and John Wallis, *Violence and Social Orders: A Conceptual Framework for Interpreting Recorded Human History* (North, Wallis, and Weingast 2009a). This work provides a new way of thinking about social, political, and economic organization, leading to a new appreciation for the problems of reform in developing countries.

This paper proceeds as follows. In Section 2, I summarize the North, Wallis, and Weingast perspective. In Section 3, I apply this to the question about democracy and the rule of law. My conclusions follow.

[*] Barry R. Weingast is a senior fellow at the Hoover Institution and the Ward C. Krebs Family Professor in the department of political science at Stanford University. This paper draws on the author's larger project in Weingast (forthcoming).

2. The Conceptual Framework

The North, Wallis, and Weingast (NWW) conceptual framework begins with the concept of a *social order*, a framework for understanding the political, economic, and other social systems. Each social order handles issues of violence, institutions, and organizations in different ways. A major premise of the approach is that all human societies fall into one of three social orders. The social orders differ in how they solve the problem of violence and how they treat organizations. The *hunter-gatherer society* reaches back to the beginnings of human history and involves a social organization of small groups, typically around twenty-five but sometimes as large as two hundred. This social order will not concern us. The *limited access order* or *natural state* arose with the beginnings of civilization between five and ten thousand years ago and includes all historical hierarchical societies and most of those on the planet today. The *open access order* is a relatively new form of social organization, arising about 150 to 200 years ago and includes two to three dozen societies today. I discuss the second and third social orders in turn.

2.1 The Logic of the Natural State

The natural state or limited access order solves the problem of violence by creating rents. It grants various privileges to powerful individuals and groups. For example, these groups may gain monopoly privileges over trade, the right to hold a market, a local monopoly on the right to mill grain, or the monopoly right to open a bank. The central logic of the natural state is this: because fighting lowers the flow of rents from their privileges, granting privileges to those with access to violence gives them an incentive to cooperate instead of fight.

Moreover, natural states must exhibit a balance between a group's power and privileges. Failing to create this balance risks violence. If a group believes its privileges are too small relative to its power, it will be tempted to use that power to take greater privileges. We call the limited access order the "natural state" because until the last two hundred years, it was the only way to organize a hierarchical society. It remains today the dominant form of social organization, covering all but two or three dozen states.

An important feature of the natural state is limited access—restrictions to elites to form organizations supported by the state. Because the political system uses rents and limits on access to sustain order, natural states cannot sustain competitive markets.

A central feature of natural states is that all relationships are personal. This means that the principal basis for enforcing exchanges is repeat-play, face-to-face interaction. Similarly, the natural state treats individuals and groups differentially; those with greater power have greater privileges and greater access to state services; those with little power may have no access to these services at all. The personal basis of natural states means that they cannot deliver policy benefits to wide classes of people based on objective or impersonal characteristics. Poverty programs may nominally attempt to provide poverty relief but instead become a form of patronage doled out by patrons to their clients or by the regime to marginal constituents. Although these states may promulgate unemployment insurance, natural states typically cannot deliver the benefits to those who have been recently unemployed.

Examples of natural states include historic states, such as the Roman Empire, the Aztecs, and medieval England. Contemporary natural states include all of Latin America and sub-Saharan Africa, most of the Middle East, and most of central, south, and Southeast Asia.

2.2 The Logic of Open Access Orders

Open access orders differ considerably from natural states. All citizens have the ability to form contractual organizations and to access the state enforcement apparatus. Open access orders therefore sustain a rich civil society with a wide variety of political, social, economic, and religious organizations. Open access to organizations also sustains competition in both the economy and the polity. People and groups are free to form and maintain political parties that compete for political power.

Because this paper is about the rule of law in natural states, I will not fully develop the logic of open access orders. Three features of these societies are critical, however, for the creation and maintenance of the rule of law. First, they support impersonal relations and impersonal exchange.[1] This means that not all

---

[1] North (1981) and Greif (2006) both emphasize the importance of the development of impersonal exchange in the growth of the West.

enforcement of exchange is through personal, face-to-face transactions. Instead, exchange can use the formal contract-enforcement apparatus of the state, making possible a far wider degree of specialization and exchange, and with it, greater wealth.

Second, open access orders have the ability to deliver public policy benefits on the basis of impersonal characteristics. Unemployment insurance, for example, can be delivered to unemployed people based on publicly specified criteria rather than being handed out by the powerful to their clients. The same holds for other social insurance programs associated with open access orders, including health insurance, old age insurance, and workers' accident insurance.

Third, all citizens have access to the courts and are subject to the rule of law. Obtaining judicial rulings does not require bribes, nor is the outcome responsive to bribes but instead follows a set of impersonal criteria set out in the law.

2.3 The Transition: The Doorstep Conditions

The NWW conceptual framework redefines the problem of economic development as the transition from a natural state to an open access order. The transition takes place in two stages: a natural state obtaining the doorstep conditions and the transition proper. For purposes of this paper's topic, I concentrate on the first stage, the doorstep conditions.

The key to the transition is that some natural states move into a position in which they can sustain incremental changes in open access. We call these the doorstep conditions.

The first doorstep condition is *rule of law for elites*. Elites in some natural states transform their privileges into a set of elite rights that are the same for all elites. They might do so, for example, because such rights are easier to enforce than a set of differing privileges. When this condition holds, elite privileges have been transformed into impersonal rights. Of course, this condition in no way implies that elites extend these rights to all people in society.

The second doorstep condition is the creation of a *perpetual state*, including the ability to sustain perpetual organizations. The idea of perpetuity is that the institutions and organizations are defined independently of the people who compose them. Political institutions, for example, do not depend on the identity of the ruler; and perpetually lived organizations are independent of the members who create them.[2] A critical feature of perpetuity is that it is necessary to bind successors. In the absence of a perpetual state, tomorrow's rulers can change the institutions, rules, rights, and privileges of elites and citizens alike.[3]

The third doorstep condition is the consolidated, political control of the military. Without such control, the other two doorstep conditions cannot hold, as is obvious from the examples of coups that can occur when this condition fails. Coups allow the new leaders to alter rules (so the second doorstep condition fails) and to terrorize citizens (so the first doorstep condition fails).

All of today's open access orders went through the transition, beginning with the first movers who completed the process in the mid-nineteenth century (Great Britain, France, and the United States), the later movers in Western Europe (also including Australia, Canada, Japan, and New Zealand). But the number of states in transition today is small, including South Korea and Taiwan and possibly some of the states in central and Eastern Europe, such as the Czech Republic, Hungary, and Poland. Virtually all other states on the planet—most developing countries—remain natural states, including all the so-called middle income countries of Argentina, Brazil, India, Mexico, Russia, and Venezuela.

3. Applying the Conceptual Framework: Why Is It So Difficult to Promote Democracy, Markets, and the Rule of Law in Natural States?

To address the paper's principal question, consider the three concepts emphasized throughout this paper: violence, perpetuity, and impersonality. As Table 1 demonstrates, natural states differ from open access orders on each of these dimensions. Consider violence. In natural states, violence potential is distributed, whereas in open access orders, violence potential is consolidated, under political control, and subject to strict rules when used against citizens. Indeed, open access orders meet the Weberian criterion that the state maintains

---

[2] Perpetual life does not imply eternal life; perpetually lived organizations can be dissolved. Rather, their life is independent of those who form them.

[3] Vladimir Putin of Russia has done this over the past several years, consolidating powers and limiting previous freedoms.

a monopoly of control over violence, whereas natural states fail on this criterion. With respect to perpetuity, political institutions in natural states are not perpetually lived but depend on the identity of the ruler and the dominant coalition. Finally, consider impersonality: natural states are highly personal, lacking the ability to treat citizens impersonally and to deliver policy benefits on the basis of objective, impersonal criteria. In short, natural states do not have control over violence, do not possess a perpetual state, and are highly personal.

Table 1: Natural States vs. Open Access Orders

Concept	Natural state	Open access order
Violence	Distributed, not controlled	Consolidated, controlled
Perpetuity	Not perpetual	Perpetual
Impersonality	Personal	Impersonal

The next step in addressing our question involves observing that too much of existing reform is based on concepts and characteristics of open access societies: that developing countries have control over violence, perpetual institutions, and can deliver impersonal policy benefits. Most reform packages implicitly assume these conditions without examination. But as we have seen, natural states fail on all three of these dimensions. To demonstrate this failure, I consider three categories of reform: rule of law, democracy, and market reform.

3.1 Rule of Law

The rule of law means different things in different contexts, and many proponents of this concept include all good things, such as democracy or specific substantive rights, in their definitions. I take a narrower approach here, focusing on the traditional elements of the rule of law (e.g., Hayek 1960; Leoni 1961). I define the rule of law to include two components: (i) the certainty of the law, so that citizens have confidence that today's rules will also be in effect tomorrow; and (ii) citizens are equal before the law so that the law is applied impersonally.

This approach to the rule of law has immediate implications for our question. First, the rule of law requires impersonality: citizens are treated based on categorical and objective indicators, not on personal ones. Second, not only must the law hold today, but it must also hold tomorrow: this embodies the concept of perpetuity. Third, violence must be controlled, for if it is not, those wielding violence can overturn the law and use force to bend others to their will.

Let's consider these points in greater detail with special attention to natural states. We can see that the rule of law requires a perpetual state: institutions must provide political officials with incentives to honor the rules today; *further,* they must provide incentives for tomorrow's rulers to do the same. In contrast, the absence of a perpetual state allows leaders to dismantle the constitution and citizen rights. Examples of leaders who have done so in natural states include Vladimir Putin in Russia, Robert Mugabe in Zimbabwe, and Hugo Chavez in Venezuela over the last several years, and Adolph Hitler in Germany during the 1930s as he consolidated his power and created the Nazi regime. More generally, in natural states, changes in the relative power of various groups or changes in the makeup of the dominant coalition typically results in changes in the institutions, laws, rights, privileges, and distribution of rents. Natural states cannot create the certainty and predictability required by the rule of law.

Second, as I have indicated, natural states are personal, not impersonal, so they have difficulty delivering policy benefits to objective classes of citizens, such as the poor or those recently unemployed. Natural states cannot create the equality of citizens before the law.

Finally, the rule of law requires that violence be under control. Yet natural states have distributed access to violence and cannot control violence. Coups, for example, are a threat in virtually all natural states. The outbreak of violence typically implies that the state cannot support today's rules, and if an opposition faction takes power through violence, the absence of perpetuity allows it to refashion institutions and laws to suit its purposes—in direct violation of the rule of law.

In short, natural states lack the conditions necessary to sustain the rule of law. It is possible to implant courts in these states, but it is not possible for them to sustain the rule of law. Indeed, most court systems in natural states are subject to considerable corruption and are another source of rents for elites.

3.2 Democracy

Why does democracy constrain political officials in open access orders but not in natural states? Many natural states sustain elections for considerable periods, including Argentina, Brazil, India, Mexico, and the Philippines. And yet it is clear that elections alone are insufficient institutions to control political officials and hold them to be responsive to citizens.

The NWW conceptual framework provides several insights into the question. Most natural states constrain elections in various ways (see North, Wallis, and Weingast 2009b). Often, they have a lack of a free press or constraints on the opposition's access to the media; for example, the radio and television are state-owned and give those in power preferential coverage.

As limited access orders, natural states constrain the ability of citizens to form organizations. In some natural states, opposition parties are illegal or the opposition leader is in jail. But even when opposition parties exist, the inability to form organizations at will means that the interests of many groups are not fully represented. For this reason, students of democracy have long emphasized the importance of a vibrant civil society for democracy (O'Donnell and Schmitter 1986; Tocqueville 1835; Putnam 1993; Widner 2001).

Perpetuity is also relevant. All successful democracies limit the stakes of power (Przeworski 1991; Weingast 1997; 2008). Democracies that fail to limit the stakes are more likely to experience coups and other sorts of extra-constitutional action. When the state threatens what people hold dear, they are willing to support coups as a means of protecting themselves. As an example, landholders in Chile in the early 1970s felt threatened by socialist president Salvador Allende's policies, including potential land redistribution, so they supported the military coup in 1973 launched by August Pinochet. Societies with credible limits on the stakes of politics therefore make coups and other forms of extra-constitutional action less likely. Credible limits, in turn, require a perpetual state, something absent in nearly all natural states.

In short, natural states may hold elections, but these institutions work differently than they do in open access orders.

3.3 Market Reform

Economists have long argued that market reform is essential for long-term economic development for developing countries.[4] They argue that reform is

---

[4] We explore the implications of the conceptual framework for economic development in NWW (2009a, ch. 7) and in North, Wallis, Webb, and Weingast (2007).

Pareto optimal—that it will make everyone better off. But economists face a problem: why have so few developing countries taken their advice? Why do most reform packages offered by international donors over the last twenty-five years fail to produce development?

The answer to these questions is that the economists are wrong; market reform will not make everyone better off. Economists miss the problem of violence, and in doing so, misunderstand the problems of development. Economists look at developing economies and see too much "market intervention," policies that grant privileges and rents to particular groups. Indeed, many proclaim these societies are rent-seeking, meaning that too many interest groups have pressed their case to the government and gained anti-competitive privileges that create rents. To this diagnosis, they recommend market reform: open access to new firms, removal of privileges, and anti-competitive government regulation.

Why does the economists' approach fail? The conceptual framework provides the answer. This approach begins with the problem of violence ignored by economists and suggests that rents, privileges, and anti-competitive regulation are not the result of stupid policymakers or greedy people. Rather, these rents arise because they are the means of forestalling the problem of violence. By granting the powerful a stake in cooperation, rents limit the problem of violence.

Into this natural state system come the economists armed with economic reform that effectively suggests dismantling the policies that create social order, the very glue of societies that maintain peace. Dismantling this system will not result in competitive markets and long-term economic growth but instead risks violence. And the threat of violence does not make everyone better off but threatens to make them worse off. For this reason, people in natural states typically resist reform.

4. Conclusions: Why Reforms Fail

The implicit model underlying most reforms is that developing countries are sick and that they need the appropriate medicine—i.e., policy reform. This perspective misperceives the problem. Natural states are not sick. These states are successful in the sense that they are structured in particular ways—including public policies structuring markets that create rents and privileges—as a means of solving the problem of violence.

Attempts to create rule of law, democracy, and market reform fail because they fail to take into account the logic of the natural state. I emphasized three central characteristics of the natural state: violence, lack of perpetuity, and lack of impersonality. All three characteristics hinder the process of reform and prevent creation of the rule of law, democracy, and markets in natural states. Put simply, these reforms cannot succeed in natural states. To affect any of these reforms, natural states must attain consolidated control over violence, a perpetual state, and the ability to treat their citizens impersonally, including providing policies on an impersonal basis. Unfortunately, these are each part of the doorstep conditions, and few natural states are close to being in a position to attain them.

The conceptual framework offers no magic bullets; no new, straightforward, or easy path emerges for development.[5] Indeed, development remains a hard problem, perhaps conceptually more difficult than before. Our perspective suggests that, before reform of the traditional type can move forward, developing countries need to provide the basis for control of violence, a perpetual state, and impersonality. Attention to these issues is necessary before natural states can develop democracy, competitive markets, and the rule of law.

References

Greif, Avner. 2006. *Institutions and the Path to the Modern Economy*. New York: Cambridge University Press.

Hayek, Friedrich A. 1960. *The Constitution of Liberty*. Chicago: University of Chicago Press.

Leoni, Bruno. 1961. *Freedom and the Law*. Los Angeles: Nash Publishing.

North, Douglass, C. 1981. *Structure and Change in Economic History*. New York: W.W. Norton.

North, Douglass, C., John Joseph Wallis, and Barry R. Weingast. 2009a. *Violence and Social Orders: A Conceptual Framework for Understanding Recorded Human History*. Cambridge: Cambridge University Press.

_____. 2009b. Violence and the Rise of Open-Access Orders. *Journal of Democracy* 20 (January): 55–68.

North, Douglass C., John Joseph Wallis, Steven B. Webb, and Barry R. Weingast. 2007. Limited Access Orders in the Developing World: A New Approach to the Problems of Development. Working Paper, World Bank.

O'Donnell, Guillermo, and Philippe C. Schmitter. 1986. *Transitions from*

---

[5] Again, we pursue the implications of the conceptual framework for development in NWW (2009a, ch. 7) and North, Wallis, Webb, and Weingast (2007).

Authoritarian Rule: Tentative Conclusion about Uncertain Democracies. Baltimore: Johns Hopkins University Press.

Przeworski, Adam. 1991. *Democracy and the Market: Political and Economic Reforms in Eastern Europe and Latin America.* New York: Cambridge University Press.

Putnam, Robert. 1993. *Making Democracy Work.* Princeton: Princeton University Press.

de Tocqueville, Alexis. 1969 [1835]. *Democracy in America.* New York: Doubleday Anchor.

Weingast, Barry R. 1997. The Political Foundations of Democracy and the Rule of Law. *American Political Science Review* 91 (June): 245–63.

_____. 2008. Self-Enforcing Constitutions: With An Application to Democratic Stability in America's First Century. Working Paper, Hoover Institution, November.

_____. forthcoming. Why Developing Countries Prove So Resistant to the Rule of Law. In Robert L. Nelson, ed., *Global Perspectives on the Rule of Law.* New York: Routledge.

Widner, Jennifer A. 2001. *Building the Rule of Law.* New York: W.W. Norton.

Institutional Transition and the Problem of Credible Commitment

Peter Boettke[*1]

I went back to graduate school with the clear intention that what I wanted to do with my life was to improve societies, and the way to do that was to find out what made economies work the way they did or fail to work. I believed that once we had an understanding of what determined the performance of economies through time, we could then improve their performance. I have never lost sight of that objective.

—Douglass North, 1993

1. Introduction

The last quarter of the twentieth century witnessed amazing political and economic transformations throughout Africa, Latin America, and Eastern and Central Europe. Between 1975 and 2000 over thirty countries were democratized. At the same time, around 1975 a transformation in economic policy ideas started to challenge the post WWII Keynesian hegemony, and free-market economic reforms were introduced to off-set economic stagnation in the democratic West and to promote economic growth in the less developed world. The track record on this democratic politics and free market policy transformation has been more mixed than one might have thought given political theory and economic theory.

* Peter Boettke is BB&T Professor for the Study of Capitalism, Mercatus Center at George Mason University and a University Professor at George Mason University.

The track record is ambiguous because while democratic politics might have been introduced in form, the substance of liberal rights and limits on state power was absent. The result has been the rise of illiberal democracy. With regard to economic policy, the story is also one of a disjoint between theory and practice. In this case, the market-oriented rhetoric was divorced from the reality of government regulation and activist policy. The IMF and the World Bank, for example, were formed during a Keynesian era to pursue Keynesian policies based on Keynesian economic theory. When Keynesian economic theory was called into question and Keynesian policies were challenged empirically, these Keynesian institutions were asked to pursue non-Keynesian policies. The so-called "Washington Consensus" emerged, which in rhetoric was supposed to promote worldwide free market reforms such as low inflation, balanced budgets, privatization, less red-tape by lowering regulation, and free trade. But in practice, the policies of these institutions are associated with macroeconomic stabilization, conditionality, and globalization. Keynesian institutions are not well constituted to pursue free market policies. Instead, what we got, even in the period of so-called market romanticism was simply an oscillation between "conservative" Keynesianism and "liberal" Keynesianism. But aggregate demand management remained the name of the game, and regulation and public sector programs were designed to address a plethora of so-called market failures.

By the late 1990s and early 2000s, tensions over globalization and debate over the failure of the Washington Consensus to generate an economic growth miracle for the less developed economies and the reforming former socialist economies of the world led to an increasing disillusionment with the laissez faire policy rhetoric of the past generation. Just as democratic transitions without liberal limits on the state resulted in illiberal democracy, economic transitions without liberal limits on the state resulted in weak growth and frustrated populations. Whenever we discuss democratic and economic reforms, it might be useful to remember that we neither desire voting just for the sake of voting or growth just for the sake of growth, but always provide instrumental value to voting and economic growth in relation to the production of effective freedoms and life improving conditions. Freedom of press, freedom of religion, freedom of association, improved sanitation, greater educational opportunities, better nutrition, wider-spread literacy, longer and less onerous lives: these are some of the things positive social change is supposed to produce. And we must recognize that many improvements to the human condition were in fact experienced by populations that for too long suffered under oppressive governments throughout Africa, Latin America, India, China, and Eastern and Central Europe. The past two decades did see progress. But there were also many examples of frustration, backtracking, and regime failure over the past ten years as well.

So why the disjoint between the rhetoric and the reality in this era that promised so much to so many throughout the world? Each case would require detailed examination in a way that is beyond the scope of any one paper, let alone a book-length treatment. Rather than promise something I cannot deliver, I will instead focus on what I consider to be an essential element in political and economic transitions of post communism—the establishment of a binding and credible commitment to liberal limits on state action. As I suggested earlier, without those liberal limits in place, democratic and economic transitions easily go astray and we end up with illiberal democracy and severely distorted and hampered market economies. The issue is not only solving a commitment problem, but also specifying the correct content to the commitment. In other words, what you are credibly committing to matters even more than whether you can commit to the policy rules required for reform.

2. What Have We Learned Since The Collapse of Communism?

In the immediate aftermath of the collapse of communism in Eastern and Central Europe and then the break-up of the Soviet Union, the focus of economic reform was on "getting the prices right." This phase lasted from roughly 1985 to 1995.

During the last phase of state socialism, struggling economies in Poland, Hungary, and even the Soviet Union attempted economic reforms that sought to allow market prices and limited use of the profit motive to address the systemic stagnation in these countries. In Poland this took the form of decentralized administered pricing and bonuses for state enterprises; in Hungary, market socialist tinkering with the price system (in the attempt to realize efficiency) was introduced in the 1960s; and even in the former Soviet Union, Khrushchev's "regionalism" and Gorbachev's perestroika involved both price reform, decentralization of decision-making, and limited introduction of the profit motive to provide incentives and mobilize the requisite information to allocate resources efficiently.

The experience in Hungary during the 1960s through the 1980s demonstrates the failure of these limited price reforms to fix the fundamental economic problems with state socialism. Free pricing actually constituted a small part of the reforms as the goods and services in the economic system were divided into those subjected to fixed prices, limited prices, and free prices. The same sort of limited reforms were introduced with respect to state enterprises. State enterprises were given more control of decision-making and basic incentive compatibility in that success was measured in "profitability" of the enterprise, but they existed in a world of soft budget constraints and lacked the market discipline that would follow from competitive entry. So-called "goulash communism" was better than traditional socialism, but still paled in comparison to the market economy in terms of production efficiency and consumer satisfaction. The experience with perestroika in the Soviet Union is similar. Market reforms were introduced in the context of state socialism but the basic ownership structure of state socialism was left in place. So again, the reforms failed to produce what was required for the economic system to become more efficient.

The failure of perestroika highlights both points about credibility that was raised in the introduction. Gorbachev introduced during his relatively short time in office (1985–1991) at least ten "radical reforms" to improve the economic situation, only to have the reforms reversed within months of introduction. A major reason for the reform measures to result in frustration was that the reforms were incentive-incompatible with basic economics. Cooperatives, for example, were permitted to freely price, but those cooperatives that priced at market prices were taxed at a higher rate than those cooperatives that priced products at the state price. As a result (as the Russian joke went at the time) a state shortage of buns and a state shortage of sausage became a sandwich sold out the backdoor. In other words, while all acts between consenting capitalist adults were supposedly freed under Gorbachev, economic actors in the Soviet Union still chose to transact in the black market rather than the newly legitimated above-ground market.

With the collapse of communist regimes in Eastern and Central Europe in 1989 and the former Soviet Union in 1991, the "getting the prices right" phase of reform began to be joined with a wide-scale recognition that prices exist within an institutional setting of private property and freedom of contract. In other words, the mantra of "getting the prices right" transformed into "getting the institutions right." At a fundamental level this was a return to the main lesson of the socialist calculation debate that prices without property were a grand illusion, as G. Warren Nutter put it. Privatization efforts throughout Eastern and Central Europe and the former Soviet Union swept through in the late 1980s and early 1990s with varying results, but mostly resulting in frustrations. Private property and freedom of contract it turned out required also a more fundamental institution—the rule of law. This led Milton Friedman to modify his advice to reforming countries from "privatize, privatize, privatize" to "privatize, privatize, privatize, provided there is a rule of law." The "getting the institutions right" message evolved over the period from 1993 to 1999. Economists paid more attention to origins of legal systems and the relationship between fundamental legal and political institutions, the institutions of policy making, and exact economic policies. As economic thinkers devoted more attention to these questions, they were led to think about the transportability of institutions across countries and cultures.

After a decade of reforms in Eastern and Central Europe and the continued frustration with foreign aid programs in Africa, along with the apparent failure of "neo-liberalism" in Latin America, the consensus on free market policy started to fracture and economists started to search for answers to the lingering puzzle of failed reform, not in terms of the price system and public policy, but in deeper social structures that produced belief systems and bonds of trust. By 2000, rather than focusing exclusively on prices and formal institutions of governance and public policy, the intellectual agenda turned to "getting the culture right." In the wake of the terrorist attacks of September 11, 2001, questions of religion and cultural preconditions for democracy and the free market took on a new sense of urgency.

This evolution of thought from prices to institutions to culture should not be interpreted as superseding what was learned during the earlier stage. But instead the stages should be viewed as the outgrowth of delving deeper into the original question of how to get an economy on track to provide generalized prosperity to the people within that economy. Generalized prosperity cannot be had without a private property market economy, but such an economy cannot be established on a wide scale without a system of governance bound by general rules and strict limits established on state action, and a country cannot meaningfully institute general rules and strict limits unless the informal beliefs and institutions of the people in question legitimate those rules and limits. It is not, as Dani Rodrick seems to suggest, "one economics and many recipes" but rather "one economics, few recipes, and even fewer favorable conditions." Transplanting the "good" rules from successful countries to aid the failing countries is a more difficult task than either humanitarian peacekeepers or military adventurists ever imagined. In this negative sense, we just have another confirmation of Hayek's (1988, 76) quip that "the curious task of economics is to demonstrate to men how little they know about what they imagine they can design."

Douglass North has argued that the general lesson we have learned from the post-communist experience (and the long march of human history toward political freedom and economic progress) is that we must see beliefs that legitimate the ends of government; limits on the stakes of politics must be in place; property and personal rights must be defined; and credible and binding commitments to respect these rights must be established (2005, 107–108). Unless these conditions are met, North argues, the transition from personal exchange to impersonal exchange relations will be thwarted and economic progress will be stunted. "The way in which beliefs → institutions → organizations → policies → outcomes evolves has led to unparalleled economic well-being and to endless disasters and human misery" (2005, 155).

To put this another way, Adam Smith argued that human beings have a natural propensity to truck, barter, and exchange, and it is this propensity that separates us from other animals. However, human history also demonstrates that we humans have a tremendous capacity to wreak havoc on one another—to rape, pillage and plunder. Progressive social change, which entails the movement from personal to impersonal exchange and the structuring of the economy and the polity as open access systems, depends on an intricate institutional matrix being in place. It is the institutions in operation as defined by the formal rules in place and the social norms that reside in the culture of the society, that ultimately will dictate whether the human propensity to "truck, barter, and exchange" dominates the darker tendency to "rape, pillage, and plunder." Human betterment follows from exchange, human misery from predation.

3. Social Cooperation under the Division of Labor

Understanding social change is made more complicated once we focus our attention on the issue of the transition from personal to impersonal exchange and what that entails for progress. To put it bluntly, we cannot have economic progress while mired in personal exchange networks. Expansion of the economic well-being of humanity requires that impersonal exchange is not only made possible but defines our daily existence. As Adam Smith famously put it, we stand in need of the cooperation of a great multitude of others for our daily survival, yet in a lifetime we have but the time to make a few close personal friends. How then are we to prevail against nature "red in tooth and claw" as frail human creatures? It is not from benevolence that we can expect our daily sustenance, the clothes on our back, or the roof over our heads. It is through channeling self-love, through exchange and the desire to profit. The butcher, the baker, and the brewer provide us with our dinner, Smith taught, not due to their benevolence, but with regard to their self-interest.

Early on in *The Wealth of Nations*, Smith actually uses the example of a common woolen coat on the back of a day laborer to communicate to his readers both the complex interdependency of exchange and production and the anonymous nature of the cooperation that must be achieved even to produce the most common products we enjoy. Explaining the emergence of this extended social cooperation under the division of labor represents the central mystery of economics, whether we are talking about woolen coats, or pencils, or automobiles, or computers. Advances in the well-being of humanity require extending specialization and exchange, and realizing those gains from trade requires both the coordination of disparate activities and the cooperation of hundreds, sometimes thousands, perhaps millions of individuals spread around the globe who will never be able to put a name or face to others in the intricate chain of economic activities yet will do their part day in and day out so that the chain is uninterrupted.

The threat to this smooth process of realizing the gains from specialization and exchange is predation. Let me distinguish between first-level and second-level predation. By first-level predation I mean the threat of predation by private actors, whereas by second-level predation I mean the threat of predation by public actors. The dilemma is that we create second-level predation only because of the way we attempt to deal with first-level predation. In our attempt to solve the problem of private predation through public means, we create the problem of public predation.

Private solutions to private predation rely on the self-regulating capacity of actors. The most common mechanisms of self-regulation are reputation and punishment. In standard treatments, these mechanisms are said to be effective only in small group settings with homogenous agents. But in such a group, the gains from exchange are limited only to the span of personal exchange networks as the gains from specialization and exchange to be had by interaction with anonymous others would be too vulnerable to predation without any recourse to be justified. To realize those gains from specialization and exchange, the theory goes, we establish institutions of governance and third-party enforcement of contracts. In most presentations, these institutions are identified with the establishment of the state—a geographic monopoly on the use of coercion. But once the state has been established to provide third-party enforcement so that anonymous exchange relations can be realized and the gains from trade and innovation can produce wealth and economic growth, the opportunity for confiscation of that wealth by public officials presents itself. The opportunism of public actors in their effort to profit through predation must be curtailed. It is this dilemma that led North (1981) to conclude that the state is both the source of economic development and the greatest threat to economic development.

4. Credible Commitment and the Paradox of Government

"The key to political order," North (2005, 107) writes, "is the establishment of credible bounds on the behavior of political officials." Private predation that is unabated may thwart economic progress by curtailing the progression from personal exchange networks to the extended order of impersonal exchange and realizing the gains from specialization, exchange, and social cooperation under the division of labor. But public predation has the potential to destroy an otherwise healthy and wealthy economy. To put it another way, if the discipline of economics is to explain the wealth and poverty of nations, then the explanation is to be found not in geography or in natural resource abundance or even in the character of the people, but instead in the fundamental institutions of governance that curb the predatory proclivities of man.[1]

If we successfully limit predation between private actors, then the gains from exchange and the gains from innovation are powerful enough to put any country on the path to prosperity. If we fail to limit the predatory behavior of public actors, even the most advantaged country in terms of location, resources and people will be mired in poverty and squalor. But, if, and only if, we are successful

---

[1] Just a note of clarification, this does translate into specific public policies as well—inflation is confiscatory, so a regime that sought to curb predation would fight against inflation, and a similar story could be told about taxation, public debt, regulation, and restrictions on foreign trade.

at establishing limits on private and public predation, then the creative powers of the citizens in that society will generate unimagined economic wealth and betterment of the human condition.

Establishing those limits on state action in a binding and credible way requires a level of constitutional craftsmanship and institutional innovativeness that has proven elusive in human history. The paradox of government has been recognized through the political history of liberalism. A government strong enough to establish a constitution is almost by definition strong enough to break the constitutional bindings anytime it desires for political expediency. The tying of the rulers' hands in politics appears to be much more difficult than Homer's depiction of tying Ulysses to the mast and putting wax in his sailors ears so he could both hear the call of the Sirens yet successfully navigate the passage without destroying the ship. The parable of Ulysses and the Sirens does capture the self-constraining behavior that is required, but in the world of politics Ulysses is also always left in possession of a knife in his hands to cut through the rope.

But in addition to the problem of credibly binding the rulers' hands, in the transition and developing countries context, the rulers must also signal specific content to the actors in the economy who have experienced public predation by the state far greater than the private predation the state was created to ward off. In the former Soviet Union, for example, the citizens had in fact heard many times before that reforms were being introduced that would grant them more freedom in economic and political life, only to have those promises broken almost as soon as they were uttered. Russian citizens referred to the "Big Lie" to describe the relationships between the citizen and the state. So rulers must not only establish credible bounds on their behavior, they must do so in a manner that credibly signals to citizens that this time they will keep their promise.

Credible commitments to curb predation are more likely to be established in high trust societies. In low trust societies, the societies that are struggling to realize the gains from trade and gains from innovation precisely because of the prevalence of predation, will have the most difficult time establishing credible commitments and signaling the content of that commitment in a way that solicits confidence that promises will be kept. Constitutions understood to be written figuratively on a word processor, for example, are not very effective constitutions. Neither were ones written on parchment, unless they were written on hearts and minds first.

So we have now come back again to beliefs and their role in easing the establishment of credible commitments. Binding constitutions are self-sustaining constitutions, and the self-sustaining characteristic is a function both of institutional craftsmanship and underlying beliefs. A free society works best when the need for the policemen is least. This statement is true because it is literally impossible to monitor every social transaction in a modern society. Most social intercourse goes on unaffected by cheating because the parties to the intercourse never consider doing the opportunistic act due to internal norms. In doing so, they lower the costs of enforcing the general rule of promise keeping. Work at the cutting edge of political economy from development economics to regulatory studies is examining this relationship between high and low trust societies and the effectiveness of regulation. The main lesson to be drawn so far from this literature is that in high trust societies, self-regulation is already in operation so state regulation is redundant at best, and in low trust societies, where one might argue that regulation is needed more, there are difficulties with getting state regulations to work.

To sum up what we have argued: in order to realize the great benefits of social cooperation under the division of labor, credible commitments that bound the behavior of public officials must be established; this binding of government must be done in a way that signals to citizens that promises made will be kept; and finally, the constitution being put in place must be self-sustaining both in terms of its institutional design and with respect to its consistency with the underlying belief system in that society.

5. Conclusion

The classical political economists emphasized that the source of social order was to be found in the stability of possession, transference by consent, and the keeping of promises (e.g., Hume). Smith referred to this set of institutional arrangements as the "system of natural liberty," and he often emphasized that deviations from that system would not only fail to bring wealth to nations but also could only be supported by tyrannical means. In the twentieth century, F. A. Hayek sought to restate the classical political economist argument for his age. Hayek emphasized the need to craft a constitutional order where bad men can do the least harm, and to do that, the task of the political economist was to discover the set of institutions that induce men to cooperate through their own interest and with respect to their own limited cognitive abilities.

Among political economists still working into the twenty-first century, Douglass North has probably done more than any of his peers to put institutions and ideology in the forefront of the research community in economics, politics, and the social sciences. A nice summary statement of his position is found in his essay on "The Chinese Model of Development," where he states, "The way the game is actually played is a function of the underlying intentions embodied in the rules, the strength of informal codes of conduct, the perception of the umpires, and the severity of the punishment for violating rules." Let me add that we have learned as well from Douglass North that progressive social change is not only about the shift in the rules, but also about the content of those rules to limit the predatory proclivities of man, which are nowhere as dangerous as in the geographic monopoly of coercion known as the state.

References

Hayek, FA. 1988. *The Fatal Conceit: The Errors of Socialism.* Chicago: University of Chicago Press.

North, D. C. 1981 *Structure and Change in Economic History.* New York: W.W. Norton.

_____. 1993. Autobiography. Nobel Prize.org. http://nobelprize.org/nobel_prizes/ economics/laureates/1993/north-autobio.html.

_____. 2005. *Understanding the Process of Economic Change.* Princeton: Princeton University Press.

_____. The Chinese Menu (for Development). *The Wall Street Journal*, p. A14, April 7, 2005.

Why Do Elites
Permit Reform?

John V.C. Nye[*]

Economists tend to be a cynical lot, or at least they can seem so to the general public. Contrary to common perception, your typical academic economist does not believe that only money matters, and self-interest is not equivalent to selfishness. People are as likely to be altruistic as venal, and in day-to-day life, they are probably more likely to exhibit kindness than viciousness. Yet it is always wise to bear in mind that self-interest, even of the more enlightened sort, must be given consideration in any serious analysis of human behavior. And any economic system is bound to fail were it to rely exclusively on "the kindness of strangers."

Nowhere does cynicism seem more justified and despair more commonplace than when considering the problem of human development throughout history. We often forget how fortunate we are to live in the wealthiest section of the wealthiest era in human history. Indeed, if we abstract away from the last few centuries, we would be justified in feeling that the default state of human civilization is penury. In all but the rarest of cases, total production and consumption were low and only a tiny elite could enjoy access to food, clothing, and transportation that would seem miserly in quantity and/or quality to the vast majority of the citizens of the developed world today. We get some sense of how bad things must have been when we realize that even today, most citizens of the world live on only a few dollars a day, while a substantial minority subsist on less than a dollar a day.

[*] John V.C. Nye holds the Frederic Bastiat Chair in Political Economy at the Mercatus Center and is professor of economics at George Mason University.

The fact that a few dozen of the world's nations seem to have figured out a way to configure their social structure so as to permit, even encourage, productive activity has only made a limited impact on the world's poorest nations. This has much to do with the ways in which political bargains that were made to assure stability and order prevent the kinds of laws and norms conducive to rapid growth.

Douglass North's life's work has taught the entire economics profession to pay close attention to the evolution of the institutions that structure economies and most especially to the way that the state controls and defines property rights. Because of the necessity of maintaining order to limit violence and coercion, we are faced with a fundamental conflict: any ruler strong enough to establish and enforce the rules that underlie a functioning economy is also able to abuse that power for his own benefit. Hence, in the common formulation, the ruling parties are faced with the decision to Make or Take. Thus, the success of the economy is critically dependent on the ability to constrain the ruler's force so that his promises of secure property rights and market-preserving order are fully credible.

If there were a mechanism to enforce efficient cooperation, human societies should evolve as to promote greater productivity and improved human welfare. But as noted in Nye (1997), the presence of high transactions costs combined with the distributional consequences of those with the power to coerce being unwilling to give up their perquisites suggest that open competition will not necessarily produce a welfare maximizing outcome for all. In his recent work with Wallis and Weingast, North (2009) has decided to treat the problem of force and violence more directly by analyzing how dominant elites band together to provide the privileged with a limited order that constrains conflict and allows the fruits of growth to be shared by them. On the one hand, this is an improvement on the Hobbesian nightmare that typically threatens the primitive order, but on the other hand, the limited competition demanded by the elites prevents the full flourishing of the polity and the economy, strongly constraining growth and welfare.

North, Weingast, and Wallis have identified many of the preconditions that seem to accompany countries that have been able to advance beyond what they call the Natural State to join the successful but rarer group of nations with widespread market competition and dispersed political power. At the end of the day, however, most of us do not really understand why elites ever permit reform.

It is common to discuss the problem of promoting economic development by referring to so-called failed states. Yet, as North's choice of the term "Natural State" emphasizes, the constrained order typical of most nations throughout history has strong stability properties rooted in the fact that one usually cannot displace beneficiaries of the existing order without losing the public benefits of that system. Thus the surprise is not that—judged by the standards of the most prosperous nations—nations fail to reform. The surprise is that meaningful reform is ever forthcoming.

Even in cases in which the elite are forced to step aside through revolution, one often observes the phenomenon that the new elites promote rules that are just as restrictive or else the revolutionaries are themselves ousted. This should be natural. To the extent that existing elites in a natural state are in a stable equilibrium, they will have evolved to be specialists in or to have made alliances with specialists in social control and violence. Successful revolutionaries are likely to be just as much specialists in taking rather than making. To the extent that fortuitous circumstances allow the makers to emerge triumphant, their victory will be short-lived unless they can solve the problems of control, which means allying themselves with specialists in force while finding stable ways to restrain them from taking over the state and becoming the new, unconstrained rulers.

Thus, most successful reform usually involves the participation of at least an important subset of the elites. But how is that to come about? This is the agenda that is suggested to us by current work in economic history and the new institutional economics.

To the extent that elites permit reform, it is usually because they cannot derive the benefits they desire without more widespread competition. But the most significant failure probably arises from a group's inability to preserve its long-term "class" interests.

For example, suppose that the nobility currently benefits from a restricted commercial market. High transactions costs and inefficient commerce preserve local control and monopoly rents. However, opening that market may allow beneficial economic and technological development. To the extent that such a transformation might be helpful to the nation at the expense of the future elites, such changes will take place only if the nation at large can force the current elites to change or to see that it is in their self-interest. Monopolistic elites usually have arranged the social order so that such pressures are neither easy nor advantageous; else the existing state would not have been particularly stable.

Thus, we expect them to cooperate only when they clearly stand to gain from the transition. But this is actually much harder to accomplish than would seem at first glance, even in countries that perform so poorly that arguably minor reform would lead to large gains in wealth for both the privileged and the masses. The major reason is that it is almost impossible to coordinate and create a binding agreement that permits the necessary reforms while guaranteeing the elites the maintenance of their political dominance and control. Even where compromises are structured to try to offer such assurances, they are usually less than credible. By its very nature, greater openness encourages innovation and change, which is both unpredictable and likely to affect the balance of power both among the elites and in the relations between the elites and the people at large. Even a modest change in average wealth, let alone the introduction of new markets and technologies, introduces so many uncertainties that preserving the social order while encouraging economic development is not credible. Yet in many ways, those are the "rights" that the privileged are most interested in maintaining.

It is strange that economists talk about the importance of property rights yet do not recognize that the rights that the fortunate are most interested in preserving are the rights to the maintenance of their existing lifestyle. That there are no easy ways to guarantee such rights, or that preserving such rights may be anathema to political liberalism is all the more reason why elites would resist reform and structure the rules to exclude any possibility of overturning the existing order.

Hence, it is often the case that elites commonly permit reform when they are either mistaken about the costs and benefits of a given change, or more commonly when the benefits are such that the current generation of elites—or a critical subset thereof—stands to gain at the expense of future generations. A Marxist might speak of the privileged betraying their class interests.

Yet it is striking that one of the most astute observers of this phenomenon was the great Adam Smith, who noted as much when considering the question of how Britain successfully began the transformation to being a liberal state. This insight was further elaborated on by Mokyr and Nye (2007) in considering what recent research in economic history tells us about the peculiar evolution of the British economy.

Eighteenth-century Britain was a hotbed of rent-seeking and corruption. And yet surprisingly, much of that venality was directed in such a fashion that it helped support an increase in public goods and a gradual, albeit uneven shift towards a more open, more market-oriented economy. Where seventeenth-century England had been a fragmented nation, rife with religious conflict with a monarch who periodically pushed the state to the edge of bankruptcy and oversaw a patchwork of regional markets that favored a provincial, rural aristocracy, eighteenth-century Britain gradually shifted to a more unified nation, dominated by a strong Parliament, whose elites were devoted both to promoting the public interest as well as enriching themselves. This took the form of improving commerce and navigation to the point where Britain in the late eighteenth century was increasingly an integrated single market and promoting public goods that enhanced commerce at the expense of local monopoly control.

For the Industrial Revolution to be successful, Britain had to overcome the problem of incumbent landed powers who drew their political, social, and economic strength from the existing blend of feudal customs and traditional arrangements. For example, improving landlords and entrepreneurial farmers had opportunities to innovate in agriculture and to re-arrange property rights through enclosures. These opportunities implied in turn that those who where least successful in making such experiments should abandon agriculture at considerable cost. Yet the losers in the process were unable to stop it using either legal or extralegal means. After 1750, the state had chosen sides. Although property rights remained one of the central mantras of Parliamentary rules, many of the activities of the eighteenth century British state "removed, reallocated, and in short, invaded property" (Langford 1991, 146). Property required regulation and enforcement, and in the eighteenth century, decisions were made increasingly on the basis of national interests (Mokyr and Nye 2007).

Market integration and political centralization were the critical characteristics of the British transformation. This led to some odd juxtapositions that belie the simple caricature of liberalism that is sometimes told in describing the British transition to modernity, but that is easier to comprehend when we consider the problem from the perspective of reforming elites. The same Britain that promoted some of the most important liberal reforms in world history was also the scene of one of the most astonishing expansions in the central state. At a time when most nations had difficulty raising government revenues substantially, the liberal British were successful in dramatically raising tax receipts to the point where government revenue grew some 400 percent more than GDP. Moreover, these revenues were mostly spent on foreign wars. Some were undoubtedly defensive, but most were part of a process of British expansion that made their nation the dominant imperial power on the planet. It is striking to note that Britain was at war for roughly half of the eighteenth century.

Scholars still do not understand what the costs and benefits of these wars were to the British economy. But it is almost certainly the case that such expansionism did not lead to the imperial bonanza that is sometimes claimed (cf. Huttenback and Davis 1987 for a sobering look at the true cost of empire). However, it is also the case that we cannot say for certain if—in practice—there had existed a more efficient and politically viable mechanism for protecting British interests and defending the realm. The ability to properly wage war is an essential element of a successful economy in a hostile world, and the right benchmark may not be limited and efficient warfare but a comparison between fighting "inefficiently" and wastefully versus having neither the structure, the will, nor the fiscal capacity to engage in armed conflict at all. All this is mere speculation at this point, but there can be no doubt—especially given the thrust of the recent work of North, Wallis, and Weingast—that institutional scholars will have to come to grips with the problem of armed conflict and the necessity of state control—warts and all—of the military. At any rate, the British somehow managed to hold off the dominant French, who were, by virtue of successful history and a much larger population, often regarded as the leading European military power.

Similarly, it is not well known that Britain did not become the paragon of free trade told to us in our history books till the very end of the nineteenth century. Recent work has demonstrated clearly that Britain still clung to many of the most important eighteenth-century mercantile tariffs that Adam Smith had damned in the *Wealth of Nations* well past the repeal of the Corn Laws. Indeed, it can easily be demonstrated that British average tariffs were in fact substantially higher than that of her neighbor France for some three-fourths of the nineteenth century.

Despite making claims to be a free trader, Britain did in fact retain many of her most important tariffs even after the Corn Law Repeal in the 1840s. The fact that most of the tariffs abandoned by the British were either of trivial importance or were tariffs on manufactures in which Britain had a comparative advantage has mostly gone unnoticed in the traditional historical literature (cf. Nye 2007).

It turns out that the tariffs were an integral part of the eighteenth century bargain that had been struck between the state and prominent merchant and industrial interests in Britain. In exchange for both protection from foreign competition and the preservation and encouragement of oligopolistic industry, groups like the brewers and distillers of London were willing to support and to pay much higher excise taxes on their products than had been politically feasible in the period prior to the Glorious Revolution. This political bargain was behind the dramatic and sustained rise in government revenues in the eighteenth century. In addition, these excises, which were mostly borne by the denizens of the most urbanized areas, notably London, not only enriched the central government and its politicians, but it also bought the peace that allowed a shifting of the rules to gradually disfavor rural elites by sparing the landed aristocracy large increases in the land and related wealth taxes that would normally have been necessary to sustain the British war machine (Nye 2007).

What is important to remember is that these tariffs and restrictions, which were by no means harmless nor liberal, did not cripple the evolution of the British economy because they also served to promote the free movement of goods and services within the domestic economy.

It is sometimes forgotten that the ideas surrounding the promotion of free trade were as much, if not more, about domestic free trade as about open commerce between nations. If Britain was not a free trader in the international market, Britain was able to prosper because the British were among the most vigorous promoters of domestic free trade. At a time when the French were still struggling with a variety of local taxes and regulations that restricted trade between the regions of France until the end of the nineteenth century, the British state was using its power to see to the development of an ever more efficient and unrestricted domestic market. These changes, combined with encouragement of improved transportation, mattered more for the economy than the restrictions on foreign trade, simply because foreign trade did not play a large role in the first Industrial Revolution.

If these changes were so unusual and far-reaching, how were they accomplished? As should now be clear from the thrust of my narrative, it is because the major elites benefited from commercialization and could successfully cut off those who would oppose the spread of national commerce. And in turn, success in the economy provided rents to the dominant elites, who benefited from further extensions in the form of improved transport, better national institutions, and rapid industrialization. The fact that in the long run, the rise of an advanced market system disenfranchised and indeed destroyed the basis for the aristocracy itself did not interfere with the power or the will of those who stood able to gain from the transformation in the short run.

Adam Smith recognized this very bargain (or perhaps class betrayal is a better phrase) when he noted most pointedly: "For a pair of diamond buckles perhaps, or for something as frivolous and useless, they exchanged the maintenance, or what is the same thing, the price of the maintenance of a thousand men for a year, and with it the whole weight and authority which it could give them. The buckles, however, were to be all their own and no other human creature was to have any share of them" (Smith 1776, Book 3, ch. IV). The destruction of feudal privilege was fueled by the pride and avarice of the central government.

Yet it is too easy to view this cynically. It is certainly the case that ideas played an important and critical role as well, difficult as it may be to quantify their effects. Both Joel Mokyr (2009) and Deirdre McCloskey (2006) have been pointing to changes in the view of mankind and the state as critical determinants of European success in the Enlightenment. Certainly, elites in poor nations both before and after the Industrial Revolution have found ways to enrich themselves without doing half so much good for the economy and the polity as did the British in the eighteenth and nineteenth centuries. The fact that reformist or liberal ideas could only function through a mechanism that provided rents for those in power should not really surprise us. Where ideas are completely at odds with the interests of those in authority, it is unlikely that they are to make any viable headway. But when an opportunity for change presents itself that also enriches those in strategic positions, it helps when those in power have on their menu of possibilities ideas that promote efficiency, access, and freedom as central elements of successful reform. That those who successfully managed to shepherd what is now seen as a world-changing transformation did so for not entirely self-less reasons should neither shock nor dismay us.

It only remains to be seen if the current and future generations of scholars can build on the insights of North and others to derive useful theories to allow us to formulate effective, sustainable policies that encourage elite reform—reforms that function in the world as it is, and not as we wish it to be, either in our dreams or on the blackboard.

References

Huttenback, Robert A. and Lance E. Davis. 1987. *Mammon and the Pursuit of Empire: The Political Economy of British Imperialism 1860–1912*. Cambridge: Cambridge University Press.

Langford, Paul. 1991. *Public Life and the Propertied Englishman: 1698–1798.* Oxford: Clarendon Press.

McCloskey, Deirdre. 2006. *The Bourgeois Virtues.* Chicago: University of Chicago Press.

Mokyr, Joel. 2009. *The Enlightened Economy: An Economic History of Britain 1700–1850.* New York: Penguin Press.

Mokyr, Joel and John V.C. Nye. 2007. Distributional Coalitions, the Industrial Revolution, and the Origins of Economic Growth in Britain. *Southern Economic Journal* 74(1): 50–70.

North, Douglass, John Wallis, and Barry Weingast. 2009. *A Conceptual Framework for Interpreting Recorded Human History.* Cambridge: Cambridge University Press.

Nye, John V.C. 1997. Thinking About the State. In *Frontiers of the New Institutional Economics*, eds. John Drobak and John Nye, Academic Press.

_____. 2007. *War, Wine, and Taxes: The Political Economy of Anglo-French Trade 1689–1900.* Princeton: Princeton University Press.

Smith, Adam. [1776] 1976. *An Inquiry Into the Nature and Causes of the Wealth of Nations.* Edited by Edwin Cannan. Chicago: University of Chicago Press.

The Importance of
Expectations in Economic
Development

Christopher J. Coyne[*]

1. Introduction

What factors and processes influence the wealth of nations? This is the central question addressed by Professor North and his colleagues John Wallis and Barry Weingast (NWW) (2009) in their framework for "interpreting recorded human history." In attempting to address this question, NWW develop a conceptual framework for understanding how institutions shape the organizations necessary for cooperation and economic development. While a small number of countries have been able to develop the institutions necessary for sustainable economic development, in most countries this outcome has been elusive. Moreover, our understanding of the process of institutional change and development is still in its early stages. From this standpoint, the NWW framework is a welcome and important contribution. It provides clarity to our understanding of different types of social orders and offers insights into the requirements for movement between different orders.

NWW differentiate between three distinct social orders. The first type of order, the "primitive social order," is a hunter-gather society. The second type of order is a "limited access order" or what the authors call the "natural state." The natural state is an order where political institutions restrict entry to the

---

[*] Christopher Coyne is assistant professor of economics at West Virginia University. Professor Coyne is also the North American editor of *The Review of Austrian Economics*.

economic system to create rents. These rents in turn are used by those in the political system to maintain order. The natural state has been the dominant form of social order for much of recorded human history. The third type of order is the "open access order." Open access orders, which are relatively new in terms of human history—approximately three hundred years old—are able to sustain order through open political and economic competition. In contrast to limited access orders, open access orders are fluid in that citizens are allowed to form contractual organizations—organizations where arrangements are enforced by third parties—that contribute to sustained openness and economic development. Indeed, open access orders characterize the handful of developed countries that exist today.

In addition to identifying the different types of social orders, NWW also provide the "doorstep conditions" necessary for the transition out of the natural state into an open access system. The doorstep conditions can be summarized as follows: (1) rule of law for elites, (2) perpetual forms of organizations for elites, and (3) political control of the military. In short, elites must be constrained by the law, just like citizens. This includes mechanisms for enforcing these constraints. Further, organizations must be perpetual, meaning their sustainability is not directly dependent on the current members of the elite. Finally, control of the military must be consolidated. When control is dispersed, as in many natural states, conflict between groups is the norm.

At first glance, the policy implications of the NWW framework may appear sobering—the toolkit of mainstream development economists will fail to assist limited access orders make the transition to open access orders. According to the NWW, instead of measuring development through standard metrics—e.g., per capita income, physical and human capital investment, and infrastructure investments, etc.—focus should be placed on the process of development that entails the shift from the natural state to an open access system. Positive changes in development metrics can indicate the movement of a limited access order closer to the doorstep conditions, but these changes, by themselves, do not constitute the process of development. Another important implication of the NWW analysis is that natural states are just that—natural. They are not "weak," "failed," or "dysfunctional." As a result, policies aimed at "fixing" these orders will fail because they are not broken in the first place.

When it comes to natural states, one might conclude that NWW are "*Panglossian* pessimists." Natural states are natural states and open access systems cannot be imposed from outside. Further, the current policies of the development community will be largely ineffective in the NWW view of the development process. It would seem that natural states are stuck being natural states with little that can be done to change the situation.

In contrast to this pessimistic interpretation, this essay emphasizes that the implications of NWW's analysis provide the foundations for a realistic reassessment of the constraints facing the development community in their efforts to assist natural states. Ultimate success requires understanding what can and cannot be achieved in efforts to assist natural states. From this standpoint, it is my contention that the implications of NWW's analysis should be read with optimism. In putting forth bold implications, NWW afford us the opportunity to critically reconsider the current policies and strategies employed by the development community, as well as potential alternatives to the status quo. The purpose of this essay is to take advantage of this opportunity.

The central theme of this paper is the role that expectations play in development. In the broadest sense, "expectations" refer to the views held by decision makers regarding the future state of key variables. Expectations play a key role in development efforts because they frame the activities of the development community, as well as the perceptions of indigenous politicians and citizens living in the natural state. A central issue highlighted by NWW's analysis is that the development community tries to impose the conditions of existing open access systems on limited access orders. Since the two do not mesh, given the absence of the doorstep conditions, failure is typically the outcome. This paper will argue that a failure to appreciate the role of incentives is an important contributor to these failures.

The expectations of the development community are naively optimistic because they fundamentally assume that the conditions of existing open access systems can be imposed or established in a natural state. These expectations result in specific policies toward natural states that assume the existence of the doorstep conditions. These policies, in turn, influence the expectations of politicians and citizens living within those states. The disconnect between what can actually be achieved in the natural state and the expectations created by the development community often leads to perverse outcomes and the failure of development efforts.

It is my contention that a central lesson from NWW's analysis is that movements within the natural state, as well as the establishment of the doorstep conditions necessary for development, are directly dependent on the existence of certain expectations. Many development problems involve a "collective action problem," which requires the coordination of many people. The solution to this problem requires that individuals are confident in their expectations about what others are going to do so that they can respond accordingly. Appropriate expectations are necessary to facilitate the widespread coordination required to overcome collective action problems.

Creating appropriate expectations ultimately requires understanding what is feasible within different social systems. NWW's framework provides a means for understanding what is feasible under different systems. For example, a transition from a limited access system to an open access system cannot take place absent the existence of the aforementioned doorstep conditions. In general, the relevant comparison is not the natural state to some ideal open access system but rather one natural state to another natural state. The central issue is understanding the realistic alternatives relative to the current natural state.

Discussions of development assistance often focus on the problems of the quantity of resources (Sachs 2005), incentives (Easterly 2001) or information (Easterly 2005). The recognition of the importance of expectations adds an additional wrinkle to these discussions. Development is not simply a matter of the quantity of the resources invested, as this assumes that the recipients have the incentive and information to use the resources effectively. Moreover, in addition to the incentive and information issues regarding the use of resources, the various parties involved in development efforts must hold certain expectations in order for the effort to be successful. Absent appropriate expectations, citizens and policymakers will fail to make the necessary commitment and investment required for success.

This paper proceeds as follows. The next section provides a brief history of modern development economics. It is important to understand how the subfield of development economics has evolved over time in order to understand how expectations regarding current development efforts get established. In the context of NWW's analysis, it will be argued that at the core of modern development economics is the assumption that the doorstep conditions allowing for an open access system have either already been established or can be established by exogenous forces. These expectations drive the type of development policies that are adopted. Section 3 explores the role of expectations in the process of economic development and discusses the factors influencing expectation formulation.

Particular emphasis is placed on the ability of the development community to effectively shape expectations. Section 4 concludes.

2. The Evolution of Development Economics and the Expectations of Development

In order to understand the expectations that have emerged regarding economic development initiatives, it is important to understand the evolution of development economics as a field of study. In the broadest sense, development economics focuses on understanding the causes for the economic progress or stagnation of societies.[1] Issues of economic development can be traced back to the earliest writings in economics as indicated by the title of Adam Smith's (1776) classic, *An Inquiry into the Nature and Causes of the Wealth of Nations*. However, the "modern" development economics subfield that exists today did not emerge until the 1930s (see Arndt 1981 and Bell 1987). The rise of modern development economics was due to several factors and events.[2]

The increased availability of statistics and data, which allowed for cross-country comparisons of standards of living, was a major factor in the rise of modern development economics. For example, Clark (1939) collected detailed data on the income accounts for the United Kingdom and is widely known for his work on national income estimation. The use of this aggregate data provided a means of comparing the wealth of nations and economic development. Comparisons of income and other measures of progress made differences in development clear and highlighted the failure of certain societies to develop and progress. As such, these data were used to identify the counties in need of assistance and aid.

Another important influence on the evolution of modern development economics were the global economic events starting in the late 1920s. The Great Depression in the United States led to questions regarding the stability of capitalism. These questions were further fueled by the industrialization of the Soviet

---

[1] For a detailed survey of the field, see Stern (1989).

[2] For a discussion of some of the important early literature in development economics, see Bardhan (1993).

Union through forced investment and saving. This supported the belief at the time that state planning was a critical element of the development process (see Myrdal 1956). In reviewing the early writing in development economics, Bell (1987, 825) emphasizes that "if they shared anything in common, it is a distrust of the proposition that matters [of development] can be left to the market." At the same time, the independence of former colonies led to numerous countries and societies with varying levels of development and institutional quality. These events led economists to focus on issues surrounding comparative economic systems and to further understand the factors contributing to development across societies.

A final influence was the rise of what today is known as the "international development community" in the 1940s. The development community includes international organizations that attempt to facilitate economic, legal, political, and social stability and development around the world. This includes the United Nations (UN), which was founded in 1945 to uphold international law, to facilitate international peace and security, and to promote economic and social development. The World Bank and the International Monetary Fund (IMF) also emerged from the Bretton Woods Agreement in 1944 as agencies of the UN and continue to play a critical role in international development efforts.

Several organizations within the World Bank are focused on economic development issues, while the IMF is closely involved in the global financial system and the global macro economy.[3] The creation of these organizations provided a centralized apparatus to carry out research regarding economic development across countries and to implement global programs and projects aimed at fostering economic development. Since the creation of its various elements in the 1940s, the development community has been a driving force behind international development efforts.

Several distinct trends have dominated modern development economics. In

---

[3] The World Bank Group consists of five international organizations: the International Bank for Reconstruction and Development (IBRD), the International Development Association (IDA), the International Finance Corporation (IFC), the Multilateral Investment Guarantee Agency (MIGA), and the International Centre for Settlement of Investment Disputes (ICSID). Although the World Bank Group was created as part of the United Nations system, each of the above agencies is governed by its member countries. Discussion of the World Bank and economic development typically focus on the IBRD and the IDA, since those agencies focus on issues of economic development.

the 1940s, the "investment gap" and "big push" theories emerged and became the centerpiece of development efforts. These theories were grounded in macroeconomic models that emphasized the importance of capital and savings for growth. For example, the Harrod-Domar model, which has long been used by those in the development community, assumed that growth in output is driven by investment in capital, which is a function of savings. Given this assumption, the model explains growth through levels of savings and the productivity of capital. The central prediction of the model is that growth is the result of increased savings and productive investments. This model is attractive from the standpoint that an analyst can make predications of growth and calculate the savings needed to yield a certain level of growth.

The Harrod-Domar model was the impetus for both the investment gap theory and the big push theory. As per the Harrod-Domar model, it was believed that the lack of growth in underdeveloped countries was due to a lack of saving and a lack of productive capital investments—i.e., an "investment gap." Governments and the international development community were seen as the remedy to both of these problems. Development analysts used the Harrod-Domar model to calculate the level of savings needed to achieve certain rates of growth in underdeveloped countries. This investment gap could then be filled by wealthy countries and the development community, who would provide aid to the governments of underdeveloped countries.

It was also believed that the problem of a lack of productive capital investments could be solved by a "big push" through government-coordinated investments of foreign aid in a number of sectors and industries.[4] This big-push style industrialization was often combined with mercantilist policies such as import-substitution, whereby underdeveloped countries would rely on domestic substitutes for goods they would usually import. The idea was that developing countries should promote the development of domestic industries that are typically underdeveloped or in their infancy.

The use of the Harrod-Domar model and the associated investment gap and big push policies continue to be mainstays in the development community (see Easterly 1997; 2001, 35–37). Advocates of increased aid rely on the investment

---

[4] The "big push" theory of development was put forth by Rosenstein-Rodan (1943) in one of the most influential papers in development economics.

gap logic as evidenced by Sachs (2005, 56–7), who attributes ongoing underdevelopment in the poorest countries in the world to the poverty trap. The central idea is that the income of citizens in these countries is so low that it barely covers the basic necessities required for survival. As such, they are unable to save for investment. The overall impact is that these societies are unable to accumulate the savings necessary to make capital investments to break out of the poverty trap. As a result, Sachs and others who rely on the poverty trap logic call for increased foreign aid from developed countries to fill the investment gap and assist poor countries in breaking out of the poverty trap.[5]

A second trend in modern development economics started in the 1960s. During this time, the development community began to expand its focus regarding the investment gap in developing countries. Prior to this broadening, the focus was on the lack of investment in physical capital. However, with the limited success of such investments, the development community began initiatives for increased investment in human capital as well as in physical capital. The underlying idea was that an educated populace was required to increase productivity and hence growth.

However, as Easterly (2001, 71–84) has documented, the massive investments in education over the past several decades have largely failed to achieve the desired outcomes. The reason is twofold. The first is that dysfunctional institutions in many of the world's poorest countries fail to generate an environment where citizens can utilize their education in a productive manner. With a low return on human capital investment, citizens responded by either not taking full advantage of educational opportunities or by leaving their home country after obtaining an education. In short, human capital matters, but only when there is a relatively high return on the initial investment. Second, efforts to centrally plan education investments, like all other aid efforts, neglect the difficulties associated with allocating aid to achieve the desired ends.

While investments in physical and human capital continue, the development community has coordinated around several core development principles known as the "Washington Consensus." The Washington Consensus is a list of ten policies first presented by John Williamson (1990) that were meant to represent the

---

[5] For critiques of the poverty trap argument, see Bauer 2000 and Easterly 2005.

consensus among the development community regarding reform in developing countries. Williamson's original list was expanded over the course of the 1990s to address issues associated with governance and institutional reform. The original and augmented Washington Consensus is summarized in Table 1.

Table 1: The Original and Augmented Washington Consensus[6]

Original Washington Consensus	Augmented Washington Consensus
Fiscal discipline	Corporate governance
Reorientation of public expenditures	Anticorruption
	Flexible labor markets
Tax reform	Adherence to WTO disciplines
Interest rate liberalization	Adherence to international
Unified and competitive exchange rates	financial codes and standards
Trade liberalization	"Prudent" capital-account opening
Openness to foreign direct investment	Non-intermediate exchange rate regimes
Privatization	Independent central banks/inflation targeting
Deregulation	Social safety nets
Secure property rights	Target poverty reduction

    The augmentation of the Washington Consensus reflected a broader trend in development economics—the emphasis on the importance of institutions. On the academic front, the renewed focus on institutions was driven by the work of Douglass North (1990, 1991, 2005) who reminded the economics profession that "institutions matter" for economic outcomes. Within the development community, the focus on institutions emerged from the realization that in many cases the implementation of the policies associated with the original Washington Consensus required fundamental institutional changes. The new Washington Consensus aims to prescribe best practice guidelines for institutional changes required for the effective functioning of the policies listed under the original

---

[6] Source: Rodrik 2007, 17.

Washington Consensus. The guidelines are typically used by the development community to develop a plan for carrying out the desired change and reforms in policies and institutions.

The evolution of modern development economics has created certain expectations within the development community regarding the process of development and what is required for development to occur. These expectations in turn influence policies and the expectations of leaders and average citizens operating within developing countries. Two challenges related to the expectations created by the tools used by modern development economists present themselves.

First, as NWW indicate, the formulation of development policies is based on the characteristics of existing open access societies. In other words, the policies designed to assist limited access societies are based on what has already been achieved in open access societies. Policies based on the characteristics of existing open access societies assume that developing countries either have already achieved the doorstep conditions—the rule of law, control over violence through political control of the military, and perpetual political institutions—or that they can obtain these conditions in a relatively low cost manner. This leads to an inaccurate comparison between open access and limited access orders. The relevant point of comparison for limited access orders is not what exists in open access orders; rather, the relevant comparison is what is feasible given the existing constraints in limited access orders. As both North and Weingast describe in earlier essays in this volume, when policies grounded in the characteristics of existing open access orders are implemented in limited access orders, they are bound to fail because the complementary conditions are absent.

Success in development efforts requires understanding what is feasible in natural states, including the real existing constraints. As NWW make clear, the movement to an open access society is often not feasible for limited access societies, at least not in the short run. What is more important is the movement toward the doorstep conditions that are necessary for the movement from limited access to open access.

This leads to a second issue with modern development economics and resulting development efforts. In addition to assuming that the characteristics of established open access systems can be achieved in limited access orders, it also assumes that the development community can centrally plan the implementation of these conditions. This neglects the process through which plans for development are transformed into actual outcomes. Easterly (2001, 2005) emphasizes the incentive and information issues involved in the process. In the realm of development, the best laid plans often fail because of perverse incentives and the absence of important information and feedback mechanisms.

A related and often underappreciated issue in the development process is the role of expectations in achieving buy-in from the relevant parties involved in development efforts—the development community, indigenous political leaders, and citizens. Absent appropriate expectations, those involved in development efforts will fail to coordinate their actions in a manner that contributes to ultimate success. Given this, understanding the role that expectations play in the development process is critical for understanding the ability of the development community to assist limited access societies. The next section provides further insight into the role of expectations, as well as the factors contributing to the formation of expectations.

3. Expectations and Development

3.1 The Role of Expectations

Expectations refer to the views held by individuals regarding the future state of key variables. Expectations play an important role in the process of development because many development issues involve a "collective action problem," the solution to which requires widespread coordination among a large number of people. In order to overcome this problem, individuals must be confident with what others are going to do so that they can respond accordingly. For example, in the case of property reform, individuals must expect that their rights will be enforced and respected by others. Absent this expectation, the reforms will fail to get off the ground or sustain over time.

In general, the absence of appropriate expectations regarding the actions of others makes it extremely difficult for individuals to effectively coordinate their actions. While the specifics of each development situation will differ, in each case if the expectations of the relevant players are aligned at least to some degree with the aims of the development effort, there will tend to be a greater degree of coordination and cooperation. In contrast, where expectations fail to align with the broader goals of development efforts, those efforts are more likely to fail.

By helping us understand how expectations are formed, work in the area of behavioral economics can provide insight into how expectations matter for development. Behavioral economics attempts to combine insights from psychology with economics to better understand economic behavior. Recent work in behavioral research illustrates that a critical element of expectation management is how outcomes relate to expectations. For instance, Diener (1984) and Frank (1989, 1997) conclude from their work that individuals assess their current state of affairs relative to their expectations. For example, a millionaire who loses $100,000 in the stock market in a single day may, at least for a while, be less happy than a middle class individual who finds a $100 dollar bill on the street. The central issue is the "frame of reference," the benchmark against which an individual compares his or her current situation, which is a critical determinant of ultimate satisfaction or disappointment. Even though the millionaire is wealthier than the middle class individual in absolute terms, he is worse off relative to his initial position. His loss, relative to his frame of reference, is greater than the gain realized by the middle class individual relative to his frame of reference.

A related literature emphasizes the importance of "anchoring" (see Tversky and Kahneman 1974). Anchoring is the tendency for people to establish one piece of information—the anchor—as a baseline when making a decision. Given limited brain processing capability, people cannot compare all relevant alternatives. As such, they pick an anchor to serve as a benchmark for comparison. The anchor, in turn, is based on past experiences and the context within which the chooser acts. Schmid (2004, 39) notes that "the value of a product is evaluated on its own relative to some limited set of alternatives that are evoked in the context and framed by the environment of the particular case." This logic can be extended beyond the value of a product and applied to outcomes of various policies, including development efforts.

A central conclusion of the behavioral literature is that individuals experience improvements by doing well or improving relative to local norms, such as consuming more than in the past or relative to other individuals. What matters are outcomes relative to the "frame of reference" or "anchor." This realization can be applied to efforts to assist limited access orders. A disjuncture between expectations and outcomes is an important reason why development efforts may fail. When individuals are forced to participate in development activities that provide an outcome that is worse than they anticipated, they may very well refuse to act in a cooperative manner. The result is a failure to solve the collective action problem required for sustainable change. For example, citizens may refuse to accept or engage in reformed political institutions because the reforms fail to meet their expectations. If a large number of citizens hold this view, the widespread coordination necessary for sustainable change will not be obtained. Given this, understanding the importance of the frame of reference or anchor is critical for those in the development community in understanding and establishing expectations and carrying out development efforts.

3.2 Setting Expectations

In general, the expectations conducive to successful development will vary with the situation. In some cases, it may be better if individuals expect very little. For instance, if expectations in the country in question are modest, coordination around development initiatives will often be easier to achieve. If the populace does not expect significant development in a short amount of time, obstacles that arise may be overlooked with less resentment. If, on the other hand, citizens expect immediate development, it may be harder for the development community to achieve the desired outcome. In such instances, citizens may quickly lose patience with and refuse to support development initiatives, which means they will ultimately fail to sustain.

Where citizens' expectations are at odds with what is feasible, they will feel cheated relative to their initial expectations—i.e., their "anchor." The result may be a lack of cooperation and investment on the part of citizens. The main implication is that efforts aimed at pushing limited access orders toward the doorstep conditions requires establishing realistic expectations to ensure that citizens have the proper frame of reference.

Where development efforts require a significant commitment on the part of citizens, success requires creating high expectations that provide an incentive for citizens to make the necessary investment. For example, in order for impersonal social and economic interaction to take place, individuals must have an expectation that their property rights will be respected. Likewise, in order for citizens to participate in the political process, they must have an expectation that their political and civil rights will be protected. This indicates that a mix of both high and low expectations is needed, depending on the nature of the activity in question.

Along these lines, one can envision the following decision rule: low expectations are best concerning cases of "goodwill," and high expectations are best concerning the provision of basic necessities and the respect of basic rights. Low expectations are best when the central question for success is whether the popu-lace will blame those carrying out the development effort for every mishap. Large and grandiose plans of "goodwill" would fall into this category. For example, in the poorest of countries, promising local and rudimentary solutions to health and education issues is more realistic compared to some kind of large-scale and well-functioning education or health care system. In these cases, low expectations are important because there is the real possibility that the failure of development efforts will result in resentment and non-cooperation in future periods.

In some cases, however, higher expectations will assist the development process. For example, in the case of security and protection from violence, indi-viduals will tend to expect immediate protection. In the absence of security, the basic cooperation necessary to achieve the broader development goals will be less likely. In such instances, high expectations are preferable so that people are willing to make the investments necessary for success in the development effort.

Past experiences with both formal and informal institutions are a critical factor in how indigenous people establish expectations. This finds support in the notion of "availability heuristics," which emphasizes how people tend to evaluate perceived possibilities relative to past experiences. As Rabin (1998, 30) notes, "A pervasive fact about human judgment is that people disproportion-ately weight salient, memorable, or vivid evidence even when they have better sources of information." On a daily basis individuals rely on guideposts to coor-dinate their actions. These guideposts are often based on past experiences or interactions with others. Driving on a specific side of the road is one example of widespread coordination grounded in past experiences. Similarly, meeting a friend or family member in a certain location based on past meetings is another example of this logic. In general, past experiences influence the current frame of reference utilized by individuals to make current decisions. The central point is that there is an epistemic aspect to the process of expectation formation in which past experience shapes expectations about the future by providing the raw materials necessary to frame the universe of imagined outcomes. The devel-opment community can attempt to create certain expectations, but the actual process of expectation formulation on the part of indigenous people is at least partially based on past experiences that are outside the control of exogenous policymakers.

The use of an availability heuristic can influence development efforts in a number of ways. For example, if citizens have had negative experiences with past development efforts, this will impact their frame of reference toward future development efforts. Likewise, if citizens have had negative experiences with their own domestic government, this will adversely impact expectations regarding development programs carried out through that government. Coyne and Boettke (2009) discuss the problem of credible commitment in reconstruction efforts. They emphasize that, based on historical interactions, citizens often do not trust their own governments, let alone foreign occupiers. This can slow or completely impede efforts to reconstruct conflict-torn countries. A similar logic can be extended to all development efforts.

In summary, the problem with establishing appropriate expectations is twofold. The first is determining what the ideal frame of reference should be so that citizens have an incentive to invest in a manner that contributes to the development effort. The second is the epistemic aspect of expectation formulation. The fact that development efforts involve exogenous forces raises an additional issue. In addition to ensuring that the proper incentives are in place, the development community must deal with the fact that the process of expectation formulation is embedded within an existing cultural context. The adaptive efficiency of a social system is a function of the epistemic properties of its political, legal, economic, and customary traditions and institutions (see North 2005; Boettke, Coyne, and Leeson 2008). As such, reforms must be grounded in customary practices, institutions, and expectations. Because those in the development community are outside the indigenous context where development efforts are taking place, they will often perceive and interpret the frame of reference of indigenous citizens in a manner that is different from how the actual citizens perceive their situations. Ultimate success in development efforts requires finding adequate solutions to both aspects of the expectations problem.

3.3 Implications

Expectations are important for development outcomes. But in setting expectations, the development community is constrained because of the epistemic aspects involved in the process of expectation formulation. The members of the development community cannot fully comprehend the past experiences of indigenous citizens, which are a critical aspect of the process of formulating the appropriate anchor. What does this imply for development efforts?

The decision rule put forth in the previous subsection can offer some guidance in answering this question. Recall that the proposed decision rule called for high expectations regarding basic "necessities," but low expectations regarding "goodwill." Creating high expectations around the delivery of basic necessities provides some certainty to guide the actions of citizens. With increased certainty, citizens can be confident in the basic rules of the game. This allows citizens to pursue and discover what they view as valuable within those general rules, resulting in the emergence of subsequent indigenous expectations. In other words, what is needed are simple and stable rules that provide a broad and predictable environment for indigenous people to engage in discovery. Because the proposed institutional environment is open ended, indigenous actors can discover the appropriate expectations regarding future developments.

For example, consider a situation where a development effort is aimed at reforming property rights. The best that the development community can do is to recognize the *de facto* property rights as quickly as possible and then enforce those rights once established. If property rights are well defined, and if citizens are confident that their property rights will be respected and enforced, they will then make the investment in utilizing that property in a manner that yields immediate and future benefits. We cannot know how they will use their property *ex ante*, but we can allow citizens to discover various alternative uses by providing broad and general rules that encourage discovery.

Bauer (2000) emphasizes the importance of "trader-entrepreneurs" in poor countries. These individuals are alert to small-scale trading opportunities that contribute to the movement from subsistence to exchange. He emphasizes that trader-entrepreneurs "are productive in both static and dynamic senses" (2000, 6). Not only do they serve an economic function through executing mutually beneficial exchanges, but they also habituate outward-looking norms and ideas which facilitate subsequent growth and development in a variety of markets. Along similar lines, Easterly (2005) emphasizes the importance of "searchers" in the development process. Searchers are individuals who explore solutions to problems through a trial and error process and who are subject to feedback mechanisms. In contrast to "planners," who rely on top-down plans to address problems, searchers rely on bottom-up solutions. An underappreciated benefit of searchers is that they play a key role in the endogenous formulation of expecta-tions. Given a basic and predicable environment that encourages such behavior, searchers will discover the opportunities and expectations that foster subsequent development. Returning to Bauer's insight, they will take advantage of existing opportunities but also create new opportunities as well.

As another example of the importance of broad and stable rules, consider the work of Chamlee-Wright and Storr (2009) regarding the rebuilding of communities in New Orleans after Hurricane Katrina. They find that public policy designed to help Katrina victims often created uncertainty regarding whether citizens would return in large numbers. This uncertainty prevented private citizens from functioning as active stakeholders in their neighborhoods and slowed the overall recovery effort. In other words, the proper anchor was not established at the outset, which reinforced pessimism on the part of citizens regarding rebuilding. Given these low expectations, private citizens lacked the incentive to invest in the rebuilding process. Chamlee-Wright and Storr argue that what public policy should have done is establish general and stable rules that served as a guidepost to citizens. This would have contributed to a set of expectations encouraging citizens to act entrepreneurially while discovering what works and what does not work in the rebuilding process.

The argument being put forth here is similar to that developed by Hayek (1960) in *The Constitution of Liberty*. Hayek argued for general and stable rules so that individuals can discover what they do not already know. Civilization progresses by discovering new knowledge and by sharing that knowledge with others. Simple and open-ended rules are necessary precisely because we cannot know everything and we cannot know what will be learned in the future. Detailed rules and regulations or unstable and unpredictable rules distort or altogether stifle this learning process and therefore limit the progress of society.

The argument being put forth here differs from Hayek's in that he was mainly focused on the meta-rules governing an entire society. The argument being made here—the need for general, simple and predictable rules—is that Hayek's logic needs to be applied to even the smallest development efforts in natural state orders. The claim is not that these small-scale efforts will contribute to the wholesale movement from the limited access systems to open access systems but instead that these efforts can contribute to marginal improvements within a given natural state.

It should be noted that creating broad and stable rules is by no means a panacea. Even establishing simple rules is not always an easy task. In many cases citizens may be reluctant to commit to basic reforms, even if they involve "necessities" such as basic rights. A variety of factors, such as war and conflict or past experiences between different groups within a society, may contribute to the failure to coordinate on basic reforms. In such cases, the set of realistic actions available to the development community is severely constrained.

Where feasible, however, the best course of action for the development community is the creation of simple and stable rules that can be quickly established and enforced. For example, efforts to protect very basic property rights and to protect citizens from exploitation by members of the political elite are likely to generate desirable outcomes as compared to more grandiose development plans. Under such a scenario, indigenous citizens have the opportunity to engage in the discovery of what works and what fails to work. The creation of such rules should be viewed as a genuine "citizen-based approach" to development because it allows indigenous actors to discover, establish, and adjust their own expectations regarding future development.

4. Concluding Remarks

NWW's analysis forces us to reconsider what the process of development entails and what the development community can accomplish. The focus of this paper has been on the role that expectations play in economic development. Modern development economics establishes unrealistic expectations regarding what can be achieved in limited access orders. Specifically, the assumption that the conditions of existing open access systems can be imposed or established in a natural state neglects the real constraints that exist in these societies. This in turn leads to policies that create perverse expectations on the part of indigenous people living in limited access orders.

This essay has three main implications. The first is that expectations matter for development efforts. Without the proper expectations, indigenous citizens will fail to make the necessary investment for successful development. The result will be that the collective action problems preventing reform and change will persist.

Second, the process of setting expectations requires establishing the proper "frame of reference" or "anchor." This, in turn, involves two issues. The first is determining what the proper benchmark should be. The second is understanding how past experiences and the indigenous context influence the formation of expectations. For obvious reasons, finding a solution to both issues can be difficult, which leads to the third implication.

The best strategy for the development community is to set high expectations regarding basic necessities. Specifically, high expectations should be established around the delivery of simple and predictable rules that will allow the citizens to engage in discovery. The more detailed and complicated the rules or the plan associated with development efforts, the more likely they are to fail. Focus should be placed on making promises that can be delivered in a relatively short period of time and which allow citizens to discover that which they do not already know. Simple rules, such as enforcing fundamental property rights, delivering essential services, and providing basic protection against violence, provide the best hope for assisting natural states in the complex process of economic development.

References

Arndt, H.W. 1981. Economic Development: A Semantic History. *Economic Development and Cultural Change* 29(3): 457–466.

Bardhan, Pranab. 1993. Economics of Development and the Development of Economics. *Journal of Economic Perspectives* 7(2): 129–142.

Bauer, Peter T. 2000. *From Subsistence to Exchange and Other Essays.* Princeton: Princeton University Press.

Bell, Clive. 1987. Development Economics. In John Eatwell, Murray Milgate, and Peter Newman, eds. *The New Palgrave Dictionary of Economics, Volume 1.* New York: The McMillian Press Ltd., pp. 818–826.

Boettke, Peter J., Christopher J. Coyne and Peter T. Leeson. 2008. Institutional Stickiness and the New Development Economics. *American Journal of Economics and Sociology* 67(2): 331–358.

Chamlee-Wright, Emily and Virgil Storr. 2009. Filling the Civil Society Vacuum: Post-Disaster Policy and Community Response. *Mercatus Policy Series,* Policy Comment No. 22 (February) Arlington, VA: Mercatus Center, George Mason University.

Clark, Colin. 1939. *Conditions of Economic Progress.* London: McMillan & Co.

Coyne, Christopher J. and Peter J. Boettke. 2009. The Problem of Credible Commitment in Reconstruction. *Journal of Institutional Economics* 5(1): 1–23.

Diener, Edward F. 1984. Subjective Well-Being. *Psychological Bulletin* 95: 542–75.

Easterly, William. 1997. The Ghost of Financing Gap: How the Harrod-Domar Growth Model Still Haunts Development Economics. World Bank Policy Research Working Paper No. 1807.

_____. 2001. *The Elusive Quest for Growth.* Cambridge: The MIT Press.

_____. 2005. *The White Man's Burden.* New York: Penguin Press.

Frank, Robert H. 1989. Frames of Reference and the Quality of Life. *American Economic Review* 79: 80–85.

_____. 1997. The Frame of Reference as a Public Good. *The Economic Journal* 107: 1832–1847.

Hayek, F.A. 1960. *The Constitution of Liberty*. Chicago: University of Chicago Press.

Myrdal, Gunnar. 1956. *An International Economy*. New York: Harper.

North, Douglass C. 1990. *Institutions, Institutional Change and Economic Performance*. New York: Cambridge University Press.

_____. 1991. Institutions. *Journal of Economic Perspectives*, 5(1): 97–112

_____. 2005. *Understanding the Process of Economic Change*. Princeton: Princeton University Press.

North, Douglass, John Wallis, and Barry Weingast. 2009. *A Conceptual Framework for Interpreting Recorded Human History*. Cambridge: Cambridge University Press.

Rabin, Matthew. 1998. Psychology and Economics. *Journal of Economic Literature* 36(1): 11–46.

Rodrik, Dani. 2007. *One Economics, Many Recipes*. Princeton: Princeton University Press.

Rosenstein-Rodan, P.N. 1943. Problems of Industrialisation of Eastern and Southeastern Europe. *Economic Journal* 53 (210/211): 202–211.

Sachs, Jeffrey. 2005. *The End of Poverty: Economic Possibilities of Our Time*. New York: Penguin Books.

Schmid, A. Allan. 2004. *Conflict and Cooperation: Institutional and Behavioral Economics*. Massachusetts: Blackwell Publishing.

Smith, Adam. 1776 [1991]. *An Inquiry into the Nature and Causes of the Wealth of Nations*. New York: Prometheus Books.

Stern, Nicholas. 1989. The Economics of Development: A Survey. *The Economic Journal* 99: 597–685.

Tversky, Amos and Daniel Kahneman. 1974. Judgment under Uncertainty: Heuristics and Biases. *Science* 185: 1124–1130.

Williamson, John. 1990. What Washington Means by Policy Reform. In J. Williamson, ed. *Latin American Adjustment: How Much Has Happened?* Washington, DC: Institute for International Economics.

Designing Incentive-Compatible Policies to Promote Human Capital Development

Carolyn J. Heinrich[*]

1. Introduction

Increases in educational attainment and the acquisition of skills have been major contributing factors to productivity growth and economic mobility for more than a century. Hundreds of studies conducted around the world have consistently shown that more schooling is associated with higher individual earnings, with a 10 percent average rate of return that tends to be even higher for low-income countries (Hanushek and Woessmann 2009). It is still a matter of debate as to whether these estimates reflect accurate measurement of the causal effects of schooling, and recent research suggests that they are more likely to underestimate the true impacts, with social returns exceeding private returns due to effects on crime reduction, health, fertility, increased citizen participation, and on the growth and productivity of the economy overall.

Indeed, a major focus of economic and social policy development in the last three decades, in both developed and developing countries, has been on raising educational attainment—that is, increasing the number of years of school

[*] Carolyn Heinrich is director of the La Follette School of Public Affairs, professor of public affairs and a faculty affiliate of the Institute for Research on Poverty at the University of Wisconsin-Madison.

attended. Policy strategies have sought to address both supply-side and demand-side constraints to human capital accumulation. One of the most prominent and widely adopted of these approaches, the conditional cash transfer program, is typically described as a demand-side policy intervention, one that removes constraints to human capital development by reducing out-of-pocket expenditures (for schooling, health care, etc.) and opportunity costs (e.g., of the loss of children's labor income and time spent accessing services).[1]

In general, cash transfers are not a politically popular public policy. Cash welfare benefits have been described as "handouts" or "something-for-nothing" transfers to the poor. Traditional arguments against cash welfare are that they foster dependency and undesirable behavior. A primary objective of *conditional* cash transfer programs is to provide short-term assistance to families in poverty, while at the same time promoting investments in long-term human capital development through conditions on benefit receipt. The conditions that typically accompany cash transfers—requiring prenatal care, infant and children's health care, nutritional education, and/or minimum school attendance rates for children—are intended to change the behavior of recipients, beginning a cycle of investments that permanently change the health and well-being of poor families and break the intergenerational transmission of poverty. The coverage of these programs is vast in some countries; for example, Brazil's Bolsa Família program that began in 2003 is expected to reach over fifty million poor persons.

My early work on conditional cash transfer programs began in Brazil, in which I worked with the health and education ministries in planning evaluations of the Bolsa Alimentacao (health) and Bolsa Escola (school) programs, two predecessor conditional cash transfer programs that were subsequently integrated into the Bolsa Familia program. At the same time, I was working with the Ministry of Social Development and the Inter-American Development Bank in Argentina to evaluate another conditional cash transfer program, the Becas Estudantiles (student scholarship) program. Like Bolsa Escola, Becas Estudantiles was intended to increase the demand for schooling by reducing out-of-pocket expenditures and opportunity costs for low-income families. In both Brazil and

---

[1] Rawlings (2004) submits that the use of demand-side interventions to target assistance represents a "marked departure from traditional supply-side mechanisms such as general subsidies or investments in schools, health centers, and other providers of social services."

Argentina, increasing returns to education were contributing to widening wage gaps between those with a post-high school education and those with lower educational levels and unprecedented increases in economic inequality.[2] In Argentina in 1999, only 27 percent of nineteen- to twenty-year-olds in the lowest income quintile completed high school, whereas the comparable number for those in the top income quintile was 83 percent. The Becas Estudantiles program was distinctive, however, in that it sought to not only promote increased attendance by providing scholarships in the form of cash transfers to students' families, but to also motivate improved school performance by making continued scholarship receipt conditional on students' satisfactory performance and grade progression.

In designing public policies that are intended to shape the behavior of the beneficiaries in ways that also advance societal goals (e.g., increased productivity and growth, reduced poverty and inequality, greater civic engagement, etc.), it is essential to align the incentives of individuals with those of both public and private entities involved in the implementation and management of public programs. In addition, given the long-term transformation of national governments away from direct provision of goods and services and toward more devolved authority and decentralized public services delivery, the role of institutions in creating "incentive systems that structure human interaction" (North 2003) and the need for more highly developed institutional capacity for managing complex systems and interactions have grown. In the sections that follow, I examine the challenges of getting the incentives "right" in two different policy contexts related to human capital accumulation: the development and implementation of conditional cash transfer programs and the provision of supplemental educational services to children in poorly performing public schools.

---

[2] In Argentina, the change in the share of aggregate labor for workers with less than a high school education declined by one-third between 1974 and 2002, and unskilled workers experienced particularly large losses in both hourly wages and hours of work in the 1990s (Gasparini 2003). At the same time, Gasparini's analysis using Mincer equations (to compute wage-education profiles) showed that returns to formal education were always positive over this period, including during economic downturns.

2. The Challenge of Aligning Incentives in Conditional Cash Transfer Programs

New institutional economics suggests that the design of conditional cash transfer programs should promote self-enforcing behavior among the cash transfer recipients. At the same time, a primary challenge to successful implementation of conditional cash transfer programs has been limited institutional capacity and resources for program management on the part of governments to support a credible commitment to the programs' key provisions. In large countries like Argentina and Brazil, funding flows from the federal government to programs that are administered at the municipal level, with local government, school, and health authorities playing key roles. And as Professor North's work illuminates, institutions consist of more than the formal rules (e.g., laws, regulations, etc.), and thus, we need to also understand the informal norms and how they guide behavior and shape economic, political, and social activity. In addition, the enforcement of both formal rules and informal norms plays a crucial role in how these economic, political, and social relationships develop and evolve.

For example, in the Becas Estudantiles program, school administrators attested that, in accord with program provisions, students' records of attendance and grades influenced the duration of their scholarship receipt. Yet interviews conducted with school teachers produced anecdotal evidence suggesting that some Becas scholarship recipients were allowed to pass to the next grade even when their performance was below the minimum expected, because the teachers knew that they were very poor. In other words, teachers informally relaxed promotional standards for program beneficiaries, a phenomenon that was also observed by Joshua Angrist and colleagues in their 2002 study of school vouchers in Colombia.

This type of response to incentives generated by conditional cash transfers is of fundamental concern, as recent research suggests that *how* additional years of schooling translate into skills and how those skills relate to labor market performance are critical to economic growth and reductions in inequality (Hanushek and Woessmann 2009). In other words, although we have long used educational attainment (e.g., years of schooling completed or graduation rates) as a primary measure of the success of human capital development interventions, this measure neglects key elements of educational quality and academic achievement and obscures our understanding of the impact of human capital development policies. In Argentina, tests of student achievement were not regularly administered to all students, which precluded the measurement of students' acquisition of cognitive skills and a richer analysis of the impact of the Becas Estudantiles program.

Despite similar challenges in evaluating Brazil's Bolsa Familia program, the world's largest conditional cash transfer program, many governments worldwide have sought to emulate this program that is widely viewed as a success in reducing poverty. Informed in part by social norms, the program design requires the mother of the family to be the cash transfer recipient, because it is believed that she is most likely to invest the cash transfer in ways that will benefit the children. Receipt of the monthly transfer is conditional on child immunizations and well-baby checks and mandatory minimum school attendance for children of school age.

In fact, New York City Mayor Bloomberg explicitly modeled the city's new Opportunity NYC program on Bolsa Familia, describing it as an incentive-based strategy to increase participation in targeted activities and programs that decrease factors that contribute to poverty and long-term dependency. Opportunity NYC provides cash incentives to families in three key areas—education, health, and employment and training—for completing activities or satisfying requirements such as regular school attendance, attendance at parent/teacher meetings, improvements on standardized school test scores, having health insurance and yearly health/dental check-ups, and full-time employment (among adults).

I would argue, however, that the swift and widespread adoption of the Brazilian conditional cash transfer program model more likely reflects the political attractiveness of policies that place conditions on benefit receipt—which are presumably incentive-compatible and in the best interests of the beneficiaries—than careful consideration of the evidence on the effectiveness of conditional cash transfers. The findings from the well-studied randomized experimental evaluation of Mexico's Progesa (conditional cash transfer) program showed some evidence of the program's impact on school attendance and grade progression but not uniformly across students of all ages, and there is little information available on its impact on student achievement and human capital accumulation, short term or longer term (Skoufias and Parker 2001).

In addition, it is still an open question as to whether the conditions placed on receipt of the cash transfers actually drive any changes observed in outcomes or behavior. For all of its technical sophistication, with the use of electronic debit cards for distribution of benefits and a centralized system for monitoring compliance with conditions, the enforcement of conditions for benefit receipt in the Bolsa Familia program is highly imperfect. For example, if a report on compliance with conditions is not made by a municipality for its beneficiary families, it is not possible to sanction those who may not be in compliance, which generates incentives to disregard the reporting requirements. At the same time, approximately 15 percent of municipal councils were improbably reporting that 100 percent of school-age children in these families were in school 100 percent of the time. And the political incentives for the councils to do so were considerable. In the poor, northeastern state of Alagoas, where over half of families get Bolsa Familia, the head of Alagoas's electoral court observed that "people come to us complaining that they sold their vote to a politician and he hasn't paid them yet," referring to their anticipated monthly cash transfer from Bolsa Familia (*The Economist*, "Happy Families," Feb 7, 2008). In effect, in the absence of consistent enforcement and social norms reinforcing the program provisions, it did not pay to "cooperate."

The political benefits of the Bolsa Familia program are perhaps most clearly recognized and enjoyed by Brazil's current president Luiz Inacio Lula da Silva, who has seen increases in economic growth and reductions in income inequality that have been widely credited to Bolsa Familia and the cash it gets into the hands of the poor. For example, *The Economist* also reported that although only 30 percent of Alagoas's labor force of 1.3 million had a formal job, more than 1.5 million of its people had a mobile phone last year. This might lead one to question exactly what type of incentives the program is creating for families, and whether municipal program administrators will follow through with the program provision that requires them to discontinue the cash transfer for families that no longer meet the conditions of eligibility. In addition, the originating law set the expectation for an annual re-application for benefits by families, a provision that has been largely ignored in the administration of Bolsa Familia. I recall in 2002, in a press conference introducing the predecessor program to Bolsa Familia, Bolsa Escola, the minister of education stated that we would know that Bolsa Escola was successful when the number of families in need of the cash benefit was reduced to zero.

Unfortunately, the entrenchment of political support for a permanent Bolsa Familia benefit has come at the cost of public and intellectual interest in garnering a deeper understanding of the program's impact on economic, social, and political activity and longer-term human capital development in Brazil, i.e., beyond increasing the income of poor families. I worked with a team of scholars at the Federal University of Minas Gerais and the Brazilian Ministry of Social Development on the first phase of an impact evaluation of Bolsa Familia in Brazil, beginning in 2005, but progress on the research has been halted since 2006, and it is unclear whether the evaluation will continue. A rigorous impact evaluation of conditional cash transfer programs is essential to understanding whether the incentives are working as intended to change individual behavior in ways that improves the long-term trajectories and well-being of beneficiaries. To Mayor Bloomberg's credit, Opportunity NYC is currently being evaluated using one of the most rigorous methods possible, a random assignment experiment.

It is also worth noting that conditions on cash transfer receipt are not new to the United States—they have long been part of our cash welfare system (i.e., conditions that require participation in training and work). Like conditional cash transfer programs, in principle it seems that incentive-compatible agreements between governments and those striving to increase their skills and earnings capacities should not be difficult to establish and enforce in these programs. The rhetoric of personal responsibility, or the idea that work and training will provide a pathway out of poverty for everyone, is a simple and attractive message, but one that unfortunately collides with a difficult reality for those individuals and families who struggle to escape poverty even as they work or who cycle in and out of work and welfare. Pedro Carneiro and Nobel prize winning economist James Heckman (2002) find that the quality of the workforce has been declining since 1980, and that the labor market skills of a substantial fraction of adult welfare recipients are meager. They argue that it is far too costly to society to address the skills deficits of these adults, relative to the payoffs from investing more in human capital development at much younger ages.

Although human capital development deficits or lags are often viewed as a problem primarily of developing countries, significant gaps in human capital accumulation and skills deficiencies among U.S. youth and adult workers, as identified by Heckman and Krueger (2002), have reinvigorated education policy debates in developed countries. As they explain, a widening of skill- and education-based pay differentials, in conjunction with growing gaps in education and skills acquisition, have contributed to significant increases in economic and social inequality. The U.S. government has attempted to aggressively respond to these problems by targeting children in public schools that are underperforming or that show major gaps in student achievement by race, gender, and socioeconomic status with additional educational resources. Below I discuss the challenges of aligning incentives in a key education reform, the provision of supplemental education services.

3. The Challenge of Aligning Incentives in the Provision of Supplemental Education Services

The U.S. government has long claimed a central role in promoting human capital development primarily through its provision of public education at the K–12 level. Yet there is widespread discontent with the current public education system, which statistics suggest delivers shockingly unexceptional and uneven quality in education, even though access is universal. The most recent *National Assessment of Educational Progress* (NAEP) assessments indicate that less than one-third of U.S. fourth graders are proficient in reading, mathematics, science, and American history, and more than half of low income students cannot demonstrate basic levels of knowledge in science, reading, and history. And U.S. twelfth graders recently ranked eighteenth out of twenty-one countries in combined mathematics and science assessments.[3]

The most recent major reform, the U.S. No Child Left Behind (NCLB) Act, was signed into public law in 2002 "to close the achievement gap with accountability, flexibility, and choice." Institutional change is a central feature of the new law. In a Whitehouse report[4], President George W. Bush articulated the priorities of the act, stating that they "are based on the fundamental notion that an enterprise works best when responsibility is placed closest to the most important activity of the enterprise, when those responsible are given greatest latitude and support, and when those responsible are held accountable for producing results." The corresponding elements or priorities of the legislation include the following: holding states, districts, and schools accountable for student achievement, i.e., "parents will know how well their child is learning;" reducing bureaucracy and

---

[3] http://education-portal.com/articles/
Top_5_Reasons_Why_Public_Schools_Are_Failing_Our_Children.html

[4] See http://www.whitehouse.gov/news/reports/no-child-left-behind.html.

increasing administrative and funding flexibility for states and school districts; "empowering" parents with more information about the quality of their children's schools and offering school choice to those in persistently low-performing schools; and targeting federal funds on effective (evidence-based) practices for improving teacher and school quality.

The NCLB provision that I will discuss embodies most of these neoclassical economics elements as it aims to use market-like mechanisms and private sector involvement to improve educational opportunities for children in public schools that are performing below minimum standards.[5] Public schools that have not made adequate yearly progress in increasing student academic achievement for three years are required under NCLB to offer parents of children in low-income families the opportunity to receive extra academic assistance or to transfer to another public school. Consistent with the design and intent of the law, these interventions are implemented at the local level and draw on the private sector to offer eligible students a range of choices for supplemental educational services (SES) (e.g., free tutoring outside of regular school hours). NCLB urges states to allow for as expansive a choice as possible among non-profit, for-profit and faith-based and community organizations providers in accord with the key principle of "open market entry." Although no new federal monies are allocated along with the mandate for these institutional changes, the law obligates school districts to set aside 20 percent of their Title I funding allocation for them and to measure their effectiveness in increasing student achievement.[6] Only about 1 percent of students eligible for school choice elect to transfer to another public school, so I

---

[5] See Title I, Section 1116(e) of the Elementary and Secondary Education Act (ESEA), reauthorized by the No Child Left Behind Act of 2001.

[6] Title I federal funding, which began in the 1965 Elementary and Secondary Act, was created to allow all students an equal opportunity to receive the highest quality education possible. Through Title I, school districts can hire teachers to lower student-teacher ratios, provide tutoring for struggling students, create school computer labs, fund parent involvement activities, purchase instructional and professional development materials for teachers, hire teacher assistants, and more. The twenty percent Title I set-aside for SES and school transfers cannot be spent on administrative costs for these activities, although the district may reallocate any unused set-aside funds to other Title I activities after all eligible students have had adequate time to opt to transfer to another school or apply for SES.

will talk about the implementation of SES, which involves approximately $2.5 to $3 billion in expenditures annually (GAO 2006).

My colleagues and I at the Wisconsin Center for Education Research are studying the implementation of SES in Milwaukee Public Schools (Heinrich, Meyer, and Whitten 2008). Milwaukee Public Schools (MPS) are regrettably better known for their failures than their successes and particularly for their inequality in outcomes by race. African-American males in MPS, for example, have a graduation rate of approximately 31 percent, Hispanic males have an estimated graduation rate of 36 percent, and the white male rate of graduation from MPS is estimated to be 66 percent. In other words, the graduation rates for minorities in MPS are comparable to those that I observed for the poorest students in Argentina in 1999.

MPS is also the home of the largest publicly funded school voucher program; in the 2006–2007 school year, there were 17,410 students participating the program. Voucher schools receive $6,501 per full-time student. Less widely recognized, however, are the investments that MPS is making in supplemental educational services (tutoring) for students who enrolled in schools that have failed to make adequate yearly progress; approximately $2,000 is offered per student to use in accessing extra academic assistance outside the regular school day, and over 8,000 students were eligible for services in 2006–2007.

As described above, both the design and implementation of SES are based on neoclassical economic principles: this intervention aims to foster a competitive market, generate a wider range of choices, encourage innovative approaches to educational services delivery as providers compete for market share, and squeeze out inefficient and ineffective providers through choice and management tools that hold them accountable for performance. Stronger accountability for student performance is the primary management tool for state and local educational agencies under NCLB, which requires them to expunge SES providers that fail to increase students' academic achievement over a two-year period. Criticized by some and extolled by others, NCLB now requires annual, statewide testing to measure *all* students' mastery of academic content that meets state standards and the reporting of test results annually to the public (disaggregated within schools by gender, race, ethnicity, English proficiency, and migrant status). Thus, one might argue that state and local educational agencies have very clear-cut and widely accepted measures of SES provider performance (in the form of students' test scores) by which to evaluate program effectiveness and "discipline" the market.

A functioning market, as described by North in his work with John Wallis and Barry Weingast (2008, 45), will, in effect, help policymakers and educators solve the problem of poor educational quality, as resources are "able to move to their highest valued use, and because prices reflect marginal costs and benefits, resources can actually seek out and determine their highest valued use." Research shows that a large number of diverse organizations have newly entered the market to compete for available SES funds, with widely varying hourly rates, service costs, tutor qualifications, tutoring session length, instructional strategies, and curriculums. Local educational agencies are required to disseminate information about SES providers to students (and their parents) who are eligible for SES, and most SES providers do their own marketing as well, sending out brochures, inviting parents to presentations, and sometimes offering incentives to students to register with them. Thus, in theory, accountability and increased educational value should be realized primarily through the exercise of choice by parents and students, who in using this information, are expected to identify the best provider to meet their child's needs and sign up for services.

Research and evaluation efforts show, however, that establishing a causal relationship between SES and student achievement is particularly difficult, as is assessing the effectiveness of specific providers. First, a comparison group of students not receiving SES is essential for separating the effects of SES from other classroom and after-school activities and interventions that influence students' learning. Even then, the possibility of unobserved differences between those receiving SES and those not participating poses challenges for school districts in identifying the effects of SES. To date, beyond self-reported data and some internal performance evaluations conducted by large national providers, there is very little reliable information on the effectiveness of different organizations that are entering the market to provide SES. Nor is there adequate information on the relationship between strategies deployed by SES providers, the rates they charge, and the outcomes achieved. If estimates of provider effectiveness cannot be produced for SES vendors, how will parents and students choose providers, and how can states and school districts decide which providers should be allowed to continue to offer services and which should be withdrawn?

A question posed in North's (2003) research asks: How do people make choices "in the face of enormously complex information, imperfect knowledge, and imperfect feedback on the consequences of their actions"? The central question we are addressing in our study is: Are the SES providers with the greatest market shares also the providers who are most effective in increasing student achievement?

The findings from our study of SES in MPS suggest that relying on parents and students to check the market through their choice of providers when there is insufficient information available for judging the quality of SES vendor services is highly problematic. Recognizing this flaw in the market, some SES providers have offered students incentives to sign up for services, ranging from computers and iPods to school supplies and gift certificates. MPS students indicated in surveys that they chose providers based on the attractiveness of the incentives (i.e., iPods, computers, etc.), and early in the program, MPS became aware that students were switching providers after the start of their tutoring to get additional prizes or rewards. For example, the SES provider with the largest market share in this study period was also the vendor with the largest proportion of students (55 percent) reporting in the surveys that they had received an incentive or reward.

In general, given the limited information available to the consumers for making choices in a rapidly evolving market (i.e., with significant numbers of provider entries and exits each school year), it is not surprising that provider market shares were not highly correlated with the estimates of provider performance or other vendor characteristics in our study. Our analysis also showed little relationship between hourly rates charged by SES providers, the number of SES sessions typically offered to students, total SES hours attended by students, and provider performance in increasing student achievement. Clearly, this is not a functioning market as described by neoclassical economic theory, nor is it what NCLB intended.

The difficulties of attributing changes in student achievement to a particular school reform effort or intervention, in the absence of a random assignment evaluation, have plagued education reform efforts worldwide. In countries with fewer resources and less sophisticated systems for data collection and monitoring, these problems are enormously challenging. In a conference on incentives in education, I compared performance evaluation of city services such as street cleaning and garbage collection to the challenges of performance measurement and attribution in education. I remarked that unlike New York City's approach to photographing city streets and rating their cleanliness, we cannot take a photograph of a classroom and assess whether students have realized gains in learning.

A colleague from India at the same conference interjected that taking photos of classrooms in India is exactly what they are doing, just to verify that the teachers are reporting to the classrooms![7]

I also learned in part from my research in Honduras that just sending more money and supplies to developing countries is not the answer, just as the work of Eric Hanushek and colleagues has suggested that the level of per student spending on education in the United States bears little relationship to student achievement.[8] A World Bank country manager in Honduras described storage facilities full of supplies for schools that were not being used, while students were still attending (on average) less than 80 of the expected 180 days of schooling each year, often because they could not count on a teacher being present to meet and teach them in the classroom. Clearly, the need for improved incentives and greater institutional capacity for managing resources is critical to overcoming such barriers to increasing human capital accumulation.

4. Conclusion

The consistent and long-standing findings on the sizeable returns to human capital development, particularly investments made at a young age, reinforce that we must persist in our design of policies to increase the effectiveness of public investments in early education and human development. Although school enrollment rates are high now just about everywhere we look across the globe, the quality of education and skill levels of the workforce are incredibly uneven, even within developed countries, and there is considerable progress to be made.[9]

Our experiences to date with conditional cash transfer programs and other policies to increase human capital and skills development no doubt underscore

---

[7] One study found that one-third of Indian school headmasters were absent at the time of the researchers' visit (The PROBE team, 1999).

[8] According to the U. S. Department of Education, public schools receive an average of $9,969 per pupil, twice the average amount spent per student at private and charter schools.

[9] In Mexico, for example, primary school enrollment rates before the PROGRESA conditional cash transfer program ranged from 90 to 94 percent, and program impact estimates suggested that they increased by about 1–1.5 percent due to the program. Secondary school enrollment rates were lower on average and increased for both males and females to approximately 75–79 percent following the program.

the importance of key insights of new institutional economics that demonstrate the critical role of institutions and their incentive systems—including their historical development, political and societal acceptance, and their administration—in addressing these major public policy problems of our time. Despite the growing complexity and sophistication of our public and private organizations, along with economic, technological, and political advances over time, we are continually challenged to engineer policy changes that will reach those most in need and maximize benefits to society as well as to individuals. Indeed, this essay suggests that there is still much to be learned and tried in attempting to successfully address one of our most basic and long-standing problems, that is, how to more effectively promote human capital accumulation and fully realize its significant potential returns to improving individual health and well-being and the overall growth and productivity of the economy.

References

Carneiro, Pedro and James J. Heckman. 2002. Human Capital Policy. In James J. Heckman, and Alan B. Krueger, eds. *Inequality in America: What Role for Human Capital Policies?* Cambridge: The MIT Press, pp. 77–240.

Gasparini, L. 2003. Argentina's Distributional Failure: The Role of Integration and Public Policies. Working paper, CEDLAS, Universidad Nacional de la Plata, Argentina.

Government Accountability Office. 2006. No Child Left Behind Act: Education Actions Needed to Improve Local Implementation and State Evaluation of Supplemental Educational Services. Washington, DC: GAO Report 06-758.

Hanushek, Eric A. and Ludger Woessmann. 2009. Do Better Schools Lead to More Growth? Cognitive Skills, Economic Outcomes, and Causation. NBER Working Paper 14633, National Bureau of Economic Research, Inc.

Heckman, James J. and Alan B. Krueger. 2002. *Inequality in America: What Role for Human Capital Policies?* Cambridge: The MIT Press.

Heinrich, Carolyn J., Robert H. Meyer, and Greg Whitten. 2008. Supplemental Education Services under No Child Left Behind: Who Signs Up, and What Do They Gain? Working Paper, University of Wisconsin.

North, Douglass C. 2003. The Role of Institutions in Economic Development. United Nations Economic Commission for Europe Discussion Paper No. 2003.2.

North, Douglass C., Wallis, John J., and Barry R. Weingast. 2008. A Conceptual Framework for Interpreting Recorded Human History. George Mason University, Mercatus Center, Working Paper No. 75.

Rawlings, Laura B. 2004. A New Approach to Social Assistance: Latin America's

Experience with Conditional Cash Transfer Programs. Social Protection Discussion Paper Series No. 0416, The World Bank.

Skoufias, E. and S.W. Parker. 2001. Conditional Cash Transfers and Their Impact on Child Work and Schooling: Evidence from the PROGRESA Program in Mexico. *Economia* 2(1): 45–96.

The Economist. 2008. Happy Families. February 7.

The PROBE Team. 1999. *Public Report on Basic Education in India.* Oxford University Press, New Delhi.

North's Underdeveloped Ideological Entrepreneur

Virgil Henry Storr[*]

1. Introduction

Professor North has taught us a great deal about how institutions impact human action, about how institutional change occurs, and about which institutional matrices promote economic progress and which can retard it. Institutions, in North's (1990, 3) schema, are "the rules of the game in a society." As such, they proscribe certain activities and encourage others, "reduc[ing] uncertainty by establishing a stable (but not necessarily efficient) structure to human interaction" (ibid., 6). Institutions, North explains, have a profound effect on whether or not a society will prosper. If a society's institutions protect property rights, limit predation and encourage hard work and entrepreneurship, then that society will grow wealthy. If, instead, a society's institutions fail to protect property and encourage predation, then that society will not grow wealthy. Although establishing a stable structure, institutions that use formal constraints, such as legal statutes and contracts, or institutions that use informal methods, such as social conventions and norms, should not be thought of as static. Both formal and informal constraints can and do change. Understanding how institutional change occurs is critical for understanding if and how it is possible for societies with institutional structures that retard growth to develop

* Dr. Virgil Storr is a senior research fellow and the director of graduate student programs at the Mercatus Center, and the Don C. Lavoie Research Fellow in the Program in Philosophy, Politics, and Economics in the department of economics at George Mason University.

pro-growth institutional frameworks. Understanding institutional change is also critical for understanding how and why wealthy societies go off-track. More broadly, understanding institutional change is critical for understanding both positive and negative social change.

North has stressed that institutional change is typically piecemeal and path dependent. As he writes (1990, 6), "institutions typically change incrementally rather than in a discontinuous fashion." Although it is possible to rapidly change formal institutions (e.g., by passing a new law or overturning a previously existing statute), because informal institutions are not so easily changed, rapid shifts in the overall institutional matrix seldom occur. As he writes (2005, 62), institutional change tends to be "incremental because large-scale change will create too many opponents among existing organizations that will be harmed and therefore oppose such change." Similarly, as North writes (ibid.), "path dependence will occur because the direction of incremental institutional change will be broadly consistent with the existing institutional matrix… and will be governed by the kinds of knowledge … [that] members of organizations have invested in."

North also frequently highlights the role of entrepreneurs as agents of change whose activities within a given institutional structure can directly and indirectly alter that structure. As he writes (1990, 83), "the agent of change is the individual entrepreneur responding to the incentives embodied in the institutional framework. The sources of change are changing relative prices and preferences." Motivated by either a change in tastes or relative prices, (political and economic) entrepreneurs, North asserts, sometimes attempt to change the rules of the game in an effort to improve their bargaining position.

North (2005) has also stressed that changing people's beliefs must accompany any efforts to change the rules of a society since every institutional structure is supported by a more or less developed ideology. He has occasionally described the entrepreneurs who are seeking to change the rules of the game by changing people's minds as "ideological entrepreneurs." If ideological entrepreneurs are to successfully change formal or informal institutions, North argues, they must convince others that the ideological underpinnings of the existing institutional structure are unjust. In spite of the key role that ideological entrepreneurs play, however, the ideological entrepreneur remains an underdeveloped concept in North's work on institutional change. Beyond noting that the ideological entrepreneur works to change minds and, in so doing, changes institutions, North does not really develop the concept of the ideological entrepreneur. He does not fully describe the mechanism through which his ideological entrepreneur brings about institutional change. At times, in fact, North describes the entrepreneur as if he automatically responds to changes in relative prices and preferences rather than as an innovator or discoverer of "profit" opportunities. Additionally, North does not link his ideological entrepreneur to other forms of entrepreneurship like commercial, social, political, and institutional entrepreneurship.

Such an important concept should not remain underdeveloped. This article pieces together the few but key references to the ideological entrepreneur that can be found in North's corpus and seeks to augment them with insights about the nature of entrepreneurship found elsewhere in his work. Additionally, I draw on Kirzner and Schumpeter's work on entrepreneurship and the entrepreneurial process in an effort to develop a richer theory of the ideological entrepreneur than is found in North. Section 2, thus, outlines the role that North's ideological entrepreneur plays in bringing about institutional change. Section 3, then, discusses how the concept of the ideological entrepreneur might be developed along Kirznerian and/or Schumpeterian lines. Next, Section 4 examines North's discussions of path dependence and explores whether or not an ideological entrepreneur developed along Kirznerian and Schumpeterian lines can alter the trajectory of institutional change once path dependency has set in. Section 5 offers concluding remarks.

2. Why Did North Need to Invent the Ideological Entrepreneur?

Ideology plays an important role in North's institutional economics. Ideologies, for North (1981, 48), "are intellectual efforts to rationalize the behavioral pattern of individuals and groups." Simply put, ideologies are theories of how the world works. They can, however, vary considerably. They can be fatalistic (e.g., "life just happens") or hopeful (e.g. "hard work can lead to success"). They can be more or less developed and systematized, more or less consciously held (e.g., Marxism or classical liberalism versus the series of beliefs that "natives" use to explain life in their primitive community). They can be a collection of myths or a collection of scientific models. Although they can differ greatly in form, they all serve the same function. An ideology (i.e., a theory of how the world works) "is an economizing device by which individuals come to terms with their environment and are provided with a 'world view' so that the decision-making process is simplified" (ibid., 49). As such, they make action in a complex world possible.

Ideologies are really *shared* theories of the world. Although it is of course possible to do so, in North's schema, it is somewhat imprecise to talk about privately held or personal ideologies. "Ideologies," Denzau and North write (1994, 4), "are the shared framework of mental models that groups of individuals posses that provide both an interpretation of the environment and a prescription as to how that environment should be structured…. The mental models are the internal representations that individual cognitive systems create to interpret the environment." Because they are theories, neither ideologies nor mental models can be proven to be true. They can prove to be logically incoherent (i.e., parts of the theory are shown to conflict with other parts of the theory), inadequate (i.e., unable to explain the circumstance in which the holders find themselves), or proven false (i.e., new facts emerge which simply invalidate the theory). Consequently, we should never expect beliefs about how the world works to converge around some objectively true understanding about how the world works since it is possible that facts that contradict a person's theories might never emerge or that a person's theories might be stubborn in the face of such facts even if they ever were to emerge.

A person's cultural background and experiences, however, do shape their mental models. As such, people who have had similar life experiences and who share a common cultural background tend to share mental models. Mental models can, similarly, diverge considerably in individuals whose races, ethnicities, nationalities, classes, communities, families, sexual orientations, and/or genders differ. Ideologies (i.e., a shared framework of mental models that an individual adopts) can also influence the mental models that an individual develops. Of course a person's cultural background and experiences might have something to do with which ideologies she adopts, but two people whose cultural backgrounds and experiences are acutely different but who have adopted the same ideology will still have convergent mental models. The rich European Marxist and the poor African Marxist, for instance, can see and explain the world in broadly similar ways though they may have very little in common beyond their Marxism. Similarly, the classical liberal who embraces free markets because he was oppressed under communism and the classical liberal who embraces laissez faire because he grew wealthy under capitalism see the economy in similar ways even though their experiences differed radically.

That mental models can converge because of shared life experiences and ideologies is important for social stability. Absent a theory of how the world worked, people would not be able to act. Absent shared mental models or a commonly held ideology, it would be difficult to explain how and why people obey rules and choose to respect institutional barriers and prohibitions that are not in their narrow interests to follow. "While we observe people disobeying rules of a society when the benefits exceed the costs," North writes (1981, 46), "we also observe them obeying the rules when an individualistic calculus would have them do otherwise." Many people do not litter even though they would be able to get away with it. Many people do not cheat and steal even when it is very unlikely that they will be caught. Many people work hard even though any free riding on their part is unlikely to be detected. If a society's institutional matrix is to persist, members of that society must share an ideology that supports and justifies its existing structure.

Ideological change must, therefore, accompany institutional change if the new institutional structure is to stick; an ideological shift must follow, co-evolve with, or precipitate institutional change. According to North, people only change their ideology when it no longer seems to be an adequate explanation of the world. As North writes (1981, 49), "individuals alter their ideological perspectives when their experiences are inconsistent with their ideology." When an individual can no longer make sense of the world using his existing mental models and ideologies, he constructs or adopts new ones. But, as North notes (ibid.), it will take more than one anomaly (one unexplainable event) to get an individual to change his ideological perspective; "inconsistencies between experience and ideologies must accumulate before individuals alter their ideology." A series of events that run counter to a person's expectations can, thus, lead them to update their mental models and change their ideology.

Although the occurrence of repeated unexplainable events might explain the "why" of ideological shifts, it does not explain the "how" of ideological change nor does it yield any insight into which of the array of possible ideologies will come to dominate. For North, the "intellectual entrepreneurs of ideology" or "ideological entrepreneurs" can and often do play a key role in ideological change. Repeated inconsistencies between a person's experiences and her ideology will give the ideological entrepreneur an opportunity to convince her to adopt a new theory of how the world works. As North writes (1981, 65), when the existing ideology proves inadequate, "opportunities will be offered to the ideological entrepreneur

… to construct a counter ideology." Also, "an ideological entrepreneur who learns of an incoherence or a disturbing implication of the ideology could utilize this in order to help reinterpret that ideology" (Denzau and North 1994). Any would-be institutional entrepreneur must also be an ideological entrepreneur.

Nothing, of course, guarantees that an ideological entrepreneur will be able to convince others to accept his new ideology. North, however, has stressed the importance of an ideology's ethical implications in determining whether or not it will be adopted. As North writes (1981, 49), "ideology is inextricably interwoven with moral and ethical judgments about the fairness of the world the individual perceives." For instance, an ideology that points to the negative socio-economic consequences of greed will be paired with an ethos that prohibits greed. Any successful counter ideology must align with an individual's sense of right and wrong. Moreover, it must "not only provide a convincing image of the link between the specific injustices perceived by various groups and the larger system which the intellectual entrepreneurs desire altered, but," as North writes (ibid., 54), it must "also offer a Utopia free of these injustices and provide a guide to action."

North does offer a few historical examples of successful ideological entrepreneurs that might prove telling. Speaking of change in the ancient world, North writes (1981, 121), "the agents of change too were not all kings, emperors, or their agents; they included such persons as Rabbi Akiba ben Joseph and his pupil Rabbi Meier … Jesus of Nazareth; Saul of Tarsus … and Mohammed." Rabbi Akiba ben Joseph and Rabbi Meier are noted rabbinical scholars who did much to formalize Judaism. Jesus of Nazareth and Mohammed started two of the world's most popular religions. And Saul of Tarsus played a key role in spreading Christianity throughout the ancient world. Beyond these examples and a few others like Karl Marx and his popularizers and the U.S. Founding Fathers, North leaves us guessing as to who would count as ideological entrepreneurs and who would not.

Although ideological entrepreneurs play such a key role in bringing about ideological and, so, institutional change, North does not devote a lot of attention to them. He never, in fact, presents a systematic treatment of his ideological entrepreneur. We are left to guess if and how far his ideological entrepreneur can break a society out of path dependency. We are left to guess if his entrepreneur is a creative agent who brings about the creative destruction of ideologies, an individual who is alert to opportunities for ideological change and works to exploit those opportunities, or someone who automatically responds to relative price changes. Unfortunately, North often describes (ideological and other) entrepreneurs as if they are automatons. Arguably, North's ideological entrepreneur remains underdeveloped because although North's institutional economics is an improvement over neoclassical economics, particularly its introduction of ideological considerations, it nonetheless does not break free of it. The next section attempts to free the ideological entrepreneur from its neoclassical shortcomings by attempting to develop it along Kirznerian and Schumpeterian lines.

3. A More Austrian Ideological Entrepreneur?

North has become increasingly Austrian in recent years. Although he makes a favorable albeit brief reference to Hayek and Mises in *Structure and Change in Economic History* (1981), in *Understanding the Process of Economic Change* (2005), North extensively engages Hayek's writings on both the structure of the mind, the role of beliefs in shaping human choices and the dynamics of cultural evolution. In fact, North has described Hayek's *The Sensory Order* (1952) as a foundational text in cognitive science. That book, North writes (2005, 32–33), "pioneered in developing an understanding of the process of learning and the formation of beliefs long before cognitive scientists had developed connectionist theory." Similarly, North acknowledges (2005, 51) the similarity and the influence of Hayek's image of culture as "our inherited stock of knowledge" (Hayek 1960, 27) and his own view of culture as "the cumulative experience of past generations" (North 1994, 364).

North's ideological entrepreneur would similarly benefit from a greater engagement with Austrian theories of entrepreneurship (particularly Kirzner's and Schumpeter's). Kirzner and Schumpeter offer broadly complimentary views of the entrepreneur. Schumpeter stressed that the entrepreneur plays a key role in the development process. Development, for Schumpeter (1997, 68), "consists primarily in employing existing resources in a different way, in doing new things with them, irrespective of whether those resources increase or not." As such, it is a process of discontinuous change. It is a process of creative destruction where, through the "carrying out of new combinations," the economic system is consistently revolutionized. Schumpeter (ibid., 65) sees development as consisting of "(1) the introduction of a new good …, (2) the introduction of a new method of production …, (3) the opening of a new market …, (4) the introduction of a new source of supply and raw materials …, [and] (5) the carrying out the new organizations of any industry."

Schumpeter sees the entrepreneur as the star of this drama, the catalyst that sets the process of development in motion. His entrepreneur is an innovator who initiates new enterprises (i.e., "the carrying out of new combinations"). As Schumpeter writes (1976, 132), "the function of the entrepreneur is to reform or revolutionize the pattern of production by exploiting an invention." Because the entrepreneur is a pioneer who challenges (economic and perhaps even social) conventions, Schumpeter's entrepreneur is a bold, creative, visionary, and, in fact, heroic figure. He must act confidently as he ventures into unknown territory. Schumpeter compares his entrepreneur to the warrior classes of the past. The entrepreneur's role, Schumpeter writes (1976, 133), "though less glamorous than that of medieval warlords, great and small, also is … just another form of individual leadership acting by virtue of personal force and personal responsibility for success." Rather than being motivated primarily by a quest for glory and political power like the medieval warlord, however, Schumpeter's entrepreneur is primarily motivated by a desire for profits and economic power.

Kirzner, similarly, describes an entrepreneur who is at the heart of the market process and is motivated by the possibility of earning extraordinary profits. As Kirzner stresses, human beings possess less than perfect knowledge—that is, all possible means have not already been identified and all possible ends have not already been conceived. Instead, human beings live in a world of radical uncertainty and fundamental ignorance (Mises [1949] 1963; Hayek 1948, 1955; Kirzner 1973, [1979] 1983). There is much out there, as it were, to be discovered. For instance, sellers are often unable to locate the prospective buyers for their goods and services. Similarly, buyers in one area are often unaware that a good or service that they desire is available in a neighboring locality. Kirzner points out that these spheres of ignorance are arbitrage opportunities and that the entrepreneur is an individual who is *alert* to them. Kirzner's entrepreneurs look for and recognize these opportunities to buy low in one market and sell high in another. This includes recognizing that a set of raw materials, machinery, and labor can be bought/rented in factor markets and combined to make a product that can be sold at a profit in consumer markets. Kirzner (1994, 107) has described this alertness, for him a "generalized intentness upon noticing the useful opportunities that may be present within one's field of vision"—that is, an intentness on noticing unexploited profit opportunities as his entrepreneur's chief characteristic. The entrepreneur thus plays an essential role in getting buyers the goods and services that they want.

Although much has been made of the differences between the pictures of the entrepreneur painted by Schumpeter and Kirzner, there are broad similarities between the two figures. Both are driven by profit opportunities. Both also succeed by creating new products or markets. While Kirzner characterizes this as discovery and Schumpeter describes this as creative destruction, both succeed by seeing some possibility (e.g., to profitably combine factors in a particular way) that no one else has identified and attempted to pursue. Consequently, the Kirznerian and Schumpeterian entrepreneur must have similar personality traits. As Kirzner recently conceded (1999, 12), "entrepreneurial alertness, in [an] essentially uncertain, open-ended, multi-period world must unavoidably express itself in the qualities of boldness, self-confidence, creativity, and innovative ability." Both Schumpeter and Kirzner conceive of the entrepreneur as someone who must be willing to be a believer in a world of skeptics. That it takes time for some ventures to become profitable makes the entrepreneur's boldness all the more important.

Not surprisingly, Kirzner and Schumpeter's conceptions of the entrepreneur have been profitably used to discuss entrepreneurship in markets as well as non-market settings. Shockley et al. (2006) combine Buchanan and Tullock's public choice insights with Kirzner and Schumpeter's theories of entrepreneurship to build a theory of "public sector entrepreneurship." Public sector entrepreneurs, they explain, are politicians or officials who are alert to and work to exploit opportunities to earn political profits (i.e., political and bureaucratic power). Similarly, extending Kirzner's formulation, Holcombe (2002) has described political entrepreneurs as individuals who observe and act upon the predatory entrepreneurial opportunities that exist in government. And, Swedberg (2006) has developed and extended a Schumpeterian conception of social entrepreneurship, where social entrepreneurs creatively bring about social change through their activities.

Developing a Kirznerian and Schumpeterian ideological entrepreneur should therefore be possible. What, then, would a more Austrian ideological entrepreneur look like? And, how would he differ and what advantages would he have over North's ideological entrepreneur? A Kirznerian ideological entrepreneur would be alert to opportunities to advance an existing ideology that people in a particular place want but do not yet know about (i.e., to engage in ideological arbitrage). He would be alert to opportunities to sell a new ideology that better explains the world than existing ideologies. Similarly, a Schumpeterian ideological entrepreneur would be a bold innovator who created new conceptions of how the world works or combined and presented existing models of how the world works in new ways (i.e., to promote ideological development). He would work to capture the ideological marketplace, competing fiercely against other ideological entrepreneurs as well as against the weight of existing public opinion and conventions.

Although a Kirznerian and Schumpeterian ideological entrepreneur, as described above, is broadly consistent with North's "intellectual entrepreneur of ideology," there are several important advantages that the formulation above has over North's conception. First, it assigns to the ideological entrepreneur a specific and primary role in ideological and, so, institutional change. In his writings on institutional change, North has focused much less on the role of the ideological entrepreneur in changing people's beliefs and much more on the "spontaneous" changes (or lack of changes) in individuals' perceptions and beliefs that occur as a result of changes in relative prices. Second, North's ideological entrepreneur is ultimately *homo economicus* responding "automatically" and "mechanically" to opportunities to gain ideological profits. Neither Kirzner nor Schumpeter describes an entrepreneur that can be accounted for so easily within a maximizing neoclassical framework. Kirzner's entrepreneur makes genuine discoveries, and Schumpeter's entrepreneur is creative and disruptive. Third, a Kirznerian and Schumpeterian conception of the ideological entrepreneur brings to the fore a number of important questions about ideological change and the limits of the ideological entrepreneur. Most importantly, is the ideological marketplace similar enough to the real market so that we can talk as confidently about the ideological entrepreneur being an engine of ideological development and progress as we talk about the commercial entrepreneur being a source of economic development and progress? Stated another way, is successfully selling an ideology akin to successfully selling a product?

There are strong similarities between ideological and commercial entrepreneurs. It is certainly the case that between two ideologies that offer different but "equally" plausible theories of the world, the ideology that most people prefer to hold (for various reasons) will win a greater share of the ideological market. The ideological entrepreneur peddling an ideology that better satisfies the tastes of his customers will be more successful than a competing entrepreneur that is selling a less desirable ideology. Markets do a good job at ensuring that members in a society get what they want because the only way that entrepreneurs can earn profits is by satisfying customers' wants. When they fail to satisfy customers' wants they earn losses. The feedback of profit and loss is a powerful mechanism for making sure that entrepreneurs meet consumer demands. Winning converts in the ideological marketplace would be akin to winning customers in the commercial sphere. An ideological entrepreneur without any converts must alter either his message or the ideology he is peddling or bear the costs of not having any converts. Notice, however, in both spheres that it is not the "best" products (be they ideologies or economic goods) that win in the market but the products that actors believe "best" satisfies their desires. As such, it is not the theory that best accounts for how the world works that wins out in the ideological market-place but the plausible explanation of how the world works that best satisfies consumers' tastes.

Confidence that commercial entrepreneurs will actually work to satisfy consumers' desires does not only emanate from the robustness of the signals of profit and loss vis-à-vis the signals that entrepreneurs receive to guide their action in non-market contexts but also from a belief in the ability of actors to correctly assess how well a product (even an expensive and complex product) is satisfying their desires. If, instead, it was believed that individuals could be systematically and repeatedly tricked into buying products that did not in fact satisfy their actual wants or were poorer satisfiers of their actual wants, then any faith that markets deliver products that best satisfy our actual demands would be eroded. Although reality and experience places some limit on which ideologies an individual might believe, it is arguably more likely that they will adopt an erroneous theory of how the world works than it is that they would accept an erroneous theory of which drinks satisfy their thirst. Consequently, it is possible for ideological entrepreneurs to successfully peddle erroneous ideologies even when better explanations of how the world works are available.

That it is possible for erroneous but popular ideologies to persist would seem to lend credence to North's consistent emphasis on path dependence. Worldwide ideological convergence would be highly implausible. But, if ideological entrepreneurs (along the lines developed above) do in fact exist, then they could provide a way out of the lock-in that North emphasizes. They would both be a potential source of ideological innovations and also a potential source of institutional change away from the current path. Moreover, ideological entrepreneurs would be a source of both positive and negative social change.

4. The Ideological Entrepreneur as a Way of Solving the Problem of Path Dependence

North has relied on the concept of path dependence to explain why it is that some countries fail to progress even though we have known since Adam Smith the path from poverty to prosperity. As Smith (1776) outlined in *An Inquiry into the Nature and Causes of the Wealth of Nations*, "little else is requisite to carry a state to the highest degree of opulence from the lowest barbarism but peace, easy taxes, and a tolerable administration of justice." Still, many countries have not adopted Smith's simple formula. As North (1990, 112) writes, "path dependence is the key to an analytical understanding of long-run economic change." Path dependence, for him, explains how it is that economic activity in some societies failed to "evolve into the impersonal exchange essential to capturing the productivity gains that came from the specialization and division of labor" (North 1994, 364). And, as he writes, path dependence explains how societies can "get 'stuck' with belief systems and institutions that fail to confront and solve new problems of societal complexity" (ibid.). "The sources of poor performance," North explains (2005, 156), "have their origins in path dependence."

Path dependence, for North, is not simply a claim that the past affects the choices that people make in the present. It is not a modest claim about the influence of a society's cultural heritage on the beliefs and actions of its members and the institutions that they adopt. Instead, it is a description of how the dead hands of the past reach up from the grave to constrain and direct the living. It is a description of how societies get caught in vicious and virtuous cycles. As North writes (2005, 52), "path dependence is not 'inertia,' rather it is the constraints on the choice set in the present that are derived from historical experiences of the past." And, as he asserts elsewhere (1990, 98), "path dependence is a way to narrow conceptually the choice set and [to] link decision making through time."

Institutional changes tend to be path dependent (i.e., radical departures from the current trajectory of institutional change tend not to happen), North insists (2005: 59), because individuals find it difficult to radically change their beliefs for several reasons. First, shared mental models make it easier to communicate, trade, and, so, peacefully coexist with others. Adopting a new mental model could be personally costly unless some number of your fellows also adopt or can be convinced to adopt the new mental models. Stated another away, there are positive network effects related to mental models and ideologies. Second, an institutional matrix encourages the development of certain skills, kinds of knowledge, and ways of understanding the world. An institutional matrix encourages individuals to develop a particular set of lenses (i.e., ways of looking at the world) as well as a particular set of blinders (i.e., certain ways of looking at the world are obscured). Changing how you see the world, adopting an entirely new set of mental models, likely means casting off a lifetime of ideological capital. As North summarizes (ibid.), "the economies of scope, complementarities, and network externalities of an institutional matrix make institutional change overwhelmingly incremental and path dependent."

North (1990, 98) does stress that stories of path dependence should not be confused with stories of inevitability. Institutional changes do not necessarily continue along the path that previously developed. Still, when North discusses path dependence he appears pessimistic about the possibility of communities that are trapped in vicious cycles breaking free from them. And he does not appear to be terribly concerned about the possibility of communities experiencing virtuous cycles spiraling downward. Such changes are possible in North's system but are not readily explainable using North's system. As North confesses (1990, 112), "alterations in the path come from unanticipated consequences of choices, external effects, and sometimes forces exogenous to the analytical framework." What of the ideological entrepreneur that North employed in *Structure and Change in Economic History* (1981)? Arguably, he is not considered a source of "alternations in the path" because in North's system (ideological and commercial) entrepreneurs are simply maximizing agents responding more or less automatically to opportunities for ideological changes in hopes of reaping personal gain.

But, expanding people's perceptions of their choice sets is exactly what Schumpeterian and Kirznerian entrepreneurs do. An ideological entrepreneur developed along Schumpeterian and Kirznerian lines would be able to alter a society's path. An example from my research on democratization in the Bahamas will help to clarify this key role of ideological entrepreneurs in breaking societies out of path dependence.

Until the middle of the twentieth century, a small group of white businessmen known as the Bay Street Boys exerted almost total economic, political, and social control over the majority black British colony of Bahamas. They owned almost all of the major businesses in the country. They held an overwhelming majority of the seats in the local Assembly. Several of the businesses that they owned and establishments that they frequented (e.g. the Savoy movie theater, the restaurants in the British Colonial Hotel) were segregated on the basis of race. Additionally, they decided if and when Bahamian blacks would be allowed to celebrate their major cultural festivals, like Junkanoo, in the city center. The institutional matrix that existed in the Bahamas at the time was one that relegated Bahamian blacks to second class status in the colony; a set of institutions that taught Bahamian blacks that with but a few exceptions, and even then within limits, that success for them was unlikely; a set of institutions that most (white and black) Bahamians believed at the time to be legitimate.

In the latter half of the twentieth century, a group of educated black ideological entrepreneurs took over the Progressive Liberal Party (PLP), then a fledgling political party, and began to challenge the legitimacy of the institutional matrix that existed in the colony (Martin and Storr 2009). Alert to an opportunity to bring about an ideological shift amongst blacks in the colony, the rhetoric of the ideological entrepreneurs in the leadership of the PLP grew more radical and divisive and their activities grew more confrontational. They were initially met with some suspicion and a great deal of resistance. Within a few years, however, they had convinced a majority of blacks in the Bahamas that the Bay Street Boys control over the country was neither legitimate nor sustainable. Their ideological victory over Bay Street was crystallized on Black Tuesday. Protesting an attempt by the Bay Street Boys to gerrymander the constituency boundaries and ignoring a very public warning that the government would not countenance any protest, Cecil Wallace Whitfield, others in the PLP leadership, and thousands of their supporters marched to and surrounded the Assembly on April 27, 1965. Inside the Assembly, PLP leader Lynden Pindling railed against the government's attempts to silence debate, walked to the Speaker's desk, grabbed the ceremonial mace that is meant to symbolize the power of the people represented in the parliament, and threw the mace out of the window to the waiting crowd below. Less than two years after Black Tuesday, the PLP was the government of the Bahamas. The defeat of the Bay Street Boys at the polls also meant a defeat of colonialism, a defeat of segregation, and a defeat of artificial barriers to Bahamian black achievement. The ideological sea change that had to occur for the Bay Street Boys to lose political control over the colony cannot be overstated.

What is clear though is that the ideological entrepreneurs who controlled the PLP inspired a radical change in the thinking of Bahamian blacks. As a result of their efforts, Bahamian blacks altered their perceptions of their choice sets and began to see their current circumstances and their future prospects much differently than they had previously.

Other examples of these kinds of radical ideological and institutional shifts are not as rare as North suggests. Of course, they do not always lead to what we would consider positive outcomes. Hitler, for instance, was an ideological entrepreneur who was alert to the growing feeling of alienation amongst his countrymen and convinced many of them that in order for their nation to reach its destiny they needed to launch a world war and to begin systematically killing millions of Jews.

Alert ideological entrepreneurs can inspire a process of creative ideological destruction. They can alter paths, transforming virtuous to vicious circles and vice versa. Again, they can initiate positive and negative social change.

5. Conclusion

North's introduction of ideological considerations into economics is extremely important and should be viewed as a major advance in modern economics. By pushing beyond the neoclassical paradigm, he has developed a rich theoretical framework through which economists and others can make sense of a complex world and get at the most important questions in economics. By focusing on how ideology and institutions impact human action, he has brought to the fore considerations of how institutional change occurs and which set of institutions promote economic development and which stifle it. Complaining that his framework does not pay enough attention to the ideological entrepreneur (that he himself introduced) is nothing like a damning criticism of his approach. Still, it seems clear that further development of the concept of an ideological entrepreneur along Schumpeterian and Kirznerian lines could be an extremely fruitful addition to the theoretical toolkit that North has handed us.

References

Denzau, Arthur and Douglass North. 1994. Shared Mental Models: Ideologies and Institutions. *Kyklos* 47 (1): 3–31.

Hayek, F.A. 1948. *Individualism and Economic Order*. Chicago: University of Chicago Press.

_____. 1952. *The Sensory Order: An Inquiry into the Foundations of Theoretical Psychology*. Chicago: The University of Chicago Press.

_____. 1955. *The Counter-Revolution of Science: Studies on the Abuse of Reason*. London: The Free Press.

_____. 1960. *The Constitution of Liberty*. Chicago: The University of Chicago Press.

Holcombe, Randall. 2002. Political Entrepreneurship and the Democratic Allocation of Economic Resources. *Review of Austrian Economics* 15 (2–3): 143–159.

Kirzner, Israel. 1973. *Competition and Entrepreneurship*. Chicago: University of Chicago Press.

_____. [1979] 1983. *Perception, Opportunity, and Profit: Studies in the Theory of Entrepreneurship*. Chicago: University of Chicago Press.

_____. 1994. Entrepreneurship. In P. J. Boettke (ed.), *The Elgar Companion to Austrian Economics*. Northampton, MA: Edward Elgar.

_____. 1999. Creativity and/or Alertness: A Reconsideration of the Schumpeterian Entrepreneur. *The Review of Austrian Economics* 11 (1–2): 5–17.

Martin, Nona P. and Virgil Henry Storr. 2009. Demystifying Bay Street: Black Tuesday and the Radicalization of Bahamian Politics in the 1960s. *Journal of Caribbean History* 43 (1).

Mises, Ludwig. [1949] 1963. *Human Action*. New Haven, CT: Yale University Press.

North, Douglass. 1981. *Structure and Change in Economic History*. New York: W. W. Norton.

_____. 1990. *Institutions, Institutional Change and Economic Performance*. Cambridge: Cambridge University Press.

_____. 1994. Economic Performance through Time. *American Economic Review* 84 (3): 359–68.

_____. 2005. *Understanding the Process of Economic Change*. Princeton, NJ: Princeton University Press.

Schumpeter, Joseph. 1976. *Capitalism, Socialism, and Democracy*. London: Allen and Unwin.

_____. 1997. *Theory of Economic Development: An Inquiry into Profits, Capital, Credit, Interest, and the Business Cycle*. Berlin: Duncker & Humblot.

Shockley, Gordon, Roger Stough, Kingsley Haynes, and Peter Frank. 2006. Toward a Theory of Public Sector Entrepreneurship. *International Journal of Entrepreneurship and Innovation Management* 6 (3): 205–223.

Smith, Adam. 1776 [1991]. *An Inquiry into the Nature and Causes of the Wealth of Nations*. New York: Prometheus Books.

Swedberg, R. 2006. Social Entrepreneurship: The View of the Young Schumpeter. In Daniels Hjorth and Chris Steyaert, eds. *Entrepreneurship and Social Change.* Cheltenham, England: Edward Elgar, pp. 21–34.